"*Lawfare* is a polysemic term now widely used to signify deployments of the force of law for diverse ends, ends political and military, economic and social. With consummate erudition and a flair for the well-chosen example, Jaume Castan Pinos and Mark Friis Hau bring welcome conceptual clarity to the topic, providing a cogent model of the different species of legal means covered by the term. In so doing, they demonstrate that lawfare can yield ends that are sometimes lethal, sometimes laudable, sometimes lamentable, usually contentious. A very informative, important study of a phenomenon of growing significance across the world."

John Comaroff, *Professor of African and African American Studies and of Anthropology, Harvard University, USA*

"The book provides an excellent introduction to the concept and phenomenon of lawfare in its many facets. Using diverse examples from across the globe, it effectively illustrates how state and non-state actors – powerful and weak – engage in lawfare, strategically using rights and law to advance their political goals."

Siri Gloppen, *Professor of Comparative Politics, Bergen University, Norway*

"*Lawfare* is a controversial concept. Can the application of the Law be illegitimate or abusive? Jaume Castan Pinos and Mark Friis Hau have written a brief but comprehensive volume in which, with great clarity and insight, they examine the phenomenon of lawfare in all its complexity. A masterful analysis."

Ignacio Sánchez-Cuenca, *Professor of Political Science, Carlos III University of Madrid, Spain*

T0299883

Lawfare

This book develops a new conceptualisation of lawfare that recognises the polysemantic nature of the term.

Drawing on theoretical developments from legal anthropology, international relations, and social theory, the book scrutinises the multiple dimensions of this phenomenon. It illustrates the multifaceted character of lawfare with a wide range of historical and contemporary cases from across the globe and analyses the implications of actors pursuing political objectives through legal means. This includes the use of lawfare by states as a legal instrument to accomplish geopolitical objectives, domestic lawfare, or the use of legal instruments to undermine internal opposition, and state lawfare used by governments to 'protect' the state from internal territorial-secessionist challenges. Finally, the book shows that lawfare is not exclusively a tool for hegemonic actors, as it can also be used by civil society actors that aim to uphold their rights through legal instruments in asymmetric lawfare.

This book contributes to new developments in lawfare without shying away from controversy, acknowledging its sometimes-brutal efficacy as well as its potential pitfalls. The book will appeal to scholars and students of law, international relations, political science, anthropology, and sociology.

Jaume Castan Pinos is Associate Professor at the Department of Political Science and Public Management, University of Southern Denmark.

Mark Friis Hau is a postdoctoral researcher at the Employment Relations Research Centre (FAOS) at the Department of Sociology at the University of Copenhagen, Denmark.

Part of the NEW TRAJECTORIES IN LAW series
series editors
Adam Gearey, Birkbeck College, University of London
Prabha Kotiswaran, Kings College London
Colin Perrin, Commissioning Editor, Routledge
Mariana Valverde, University of Toronto

For information about the series and details of previous and forthcoming titles, see www.routledge.com/New-Trajectories-in-Law/book-series/NTL

A GlassHouse Book

Lawfare

New Trajectories in Law

Jaume Castan Pinos and
Mark Friis Hau

Routledge
Taylor & Francis Group
a GlassHouse Book

First published 2023
by Routledge
4 Park Square, Milton Park, Abingdon, Oxon OX14 4RN

and by Routledge
605 Third Avenue, New York, NY 10158

'A GlassHouse book'

Routledge is an imprint of the Taylor & Francis Group, an informa business

British Library Cataloguing-in-Publication Data
A catalogue record for this book is available from the British Library

ISBN: 978-1-032-26772-2 (hbk)
ISBN: 978-1-032-26774-6 (pbk)
ISBN: 978-1-003-28986-9 (ebk)

DOI: 10.4324/9781003289869

Typeset in Bembo
by Apex CoVantage, LLC

Contents

Acknowledgements

We would like to thank Professors John Comaroff and Ignacio Sánchez-Cuenca for their kind endorsements of this book and for providing valuable feedback, helping us to stand on the shoulders of giants.

We are supremely grateful to Sasha Juul Nielsen and Lena Marie Hybschmann for proofreading the book, in the process giving us great ideas for improving it. Thank you for your keen eyes.

We owe a debt of gratitude to Dr Steven Radil for designing the South China Sea map specifically for this book, allowing us to illustrate geopolitical lawfare in this area with pinpoint precision. We are likewise indebted to Júlia Reig at *Tall Giraffe* for designing our graphic typology of lawfare, giving clarity to our thoughts.

We are also grateful to our colleagues from the *Centre for Border Region Studies* (University of Southern Denmark) and *FAOS, Employment Relations Research Centre* (University of Copenhagen) for their support and advice throughout the process.

Last but not least, we would like to thank our editors at Routledge, Commissioning Editor Dr Colin Perrin and Senior Editorial Assistant Naomi Round Cahalin, for their assistance and expertise in preparing this manuscript for publication.

Chapter 1

Introduction

For the sake of academic honesty, we begin this book by acknowledging that lawfare is not, strictly speaking, a 'new trajectory' in law. What arguably constitutes a novelty is the new meanings that various actors are currently attributing to the term lawfare and the evolving understanding of the concept. Our conceptualisation, which follows from this, opens up for further, multiple applications of the term in different analytical contexts. We therefore follow Werner's claim that 'the meanings of terms such as lawfare are not set in stone, but rather, evolve through their use in different social practices' (2010: 62). One of the key objectives of this book is to scrutinise this multifaceted concept *in relation to* the social practices where it is applied, developing it as a novel concept with great analytical possibilities.

The semantic building blocks of the concept 'lawfare' are rather plain and unmysterious. This bicephalous term derives from blending two basic ideas: 'law' and 'warfare' (Kittrie, 2016: 6). Originally, lawfare was first coined by two Australian scholars, John Carlson and Neville Yeomans, in 1975. Unfortunately, the authors did not provide their newly created nomenclature with a comprehensive definition. In fact, the concept only appears once in their book chapter, when they point out that '[l]awfare replaces warfare and the duel is with words rather than swords' (1975). This sentence must be understood in the context of their critique of Western law, which they saw as excessively aimed at punishment (ibid.). This lack of conceptual substance has had critical consequences for the understanding and trajectory of lawfare, paving the way for different conceptualisations of the term.

According to the dominant academic understanding of lawfare, this phenomenon primarily occurs in military contexts where it is used as an instrument of defence or foreign policy (see Dunlap, 2008, 2009, 2010). This connects well with the understanding of lawfare as

DOI: 10.4324/9781003289869-1

a legal 'weapon of war' (Kennedy, 2006). In this book, we argue that such an understanding accounts for just one of the dimensions of lawfare, namely 'geopolitical lawfare'. Conversely, we view the concept as much more polysemantic and complex. Hence, we understand lawfare as a *multifaceted law-based instrument that can be used by a wide range of actors in both military and non-military contexts to pursue political objectives*. In other words, lawfare is a rich concept with multiple dimensions and, crucially, with multiple users. Our definition is deliberately inclusive in the sense that it does not challenge any of the existing, narrower conceptualisations. Instead, it is aimed at having a wider scope that incorporates – and acknowledges – different dimensions of lawfare.

The emergence of *new* types of lawfare inevitably generates a discrepancy between the dominant military-grounded definition and the very different nature and meaning of some contemporary applications. With a few notable exceptions (Comaroff and Comaroff, 2006, 2007, 2009; Gloppen, 2018), the conceptual diversity of lawfare has so far not been met with a rigorous academic conceptualisation. We contend that the new applications of lawfare are not only a popular term in contemporary societal and political debates but have rich analytical potential and terminological value. Following Anthony Giddens's (1984) 'double hermeneutic', or the mutual interpretative interplay between the social sciences and those studied, we acknowledge that just as theories help to reconstitute the social world, real-life ideas about the world are the very foundation for theoretical insights.

Similar to other concepts, lawfare is susceptible to different interpretations, applications, and transformations as the meaning of the concept mutates by virtue of social practices and political context. As McGinn eloquently puts it, 'words . . . don't have meaning nonderivatively' (2017: 82) but derive from specific contexts. For this reason, we seek to follow empirical reality – the increasing use of lawfare in geopolitical domestic, territorial, and asymmetric conflicts – to develop a scholarly conceptualisation of the term that widens its meaning and encapsulates its multifaceted and polysemantic character.

To this end, we propose a new multidimensional conceptualisation of lawfare fitting the term's current popularity and general use in society as well as its previous academic interpretations (see Figure 1.1). Our scrutiny of the multiple dimensions of lawfare is theoretically well-grounded, drawing on developments from legal anthropology, international relations, and social theory. Further, our study aims to shed light on the different uses of lawfare by considering which actors use it, in which context, and with which political objectives.

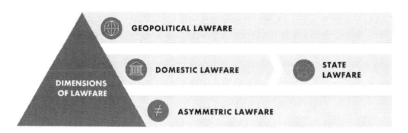

Figure 1.1 The multiple dimensions of lawfare
Source: elaborated by authors

Our first dimension of lawfare is '**geopolitical lawfare**'. This is currently the most prevalent meaning of lawfare in academia, understood as the use of legal instruments in international security and geopolitical struggles for power. It is less financially costly and more discreet than other power instruments on the international scale. Geopolitical lawfare is being increasingly incorporated into the security strategy documents of the US, the People's Republic of China, and the Russian Federation, often as a method of hybrid warfare.

The second dimension, '**domestic lawfare**', is perhaps the most potentially pernicious variant of lawfare for liberal democratic systems. We define it as the strategy, pursued by domestic political actors, of using – and often misusing – legal instruments to undermine their political opponents. This instrumentalisation of the law is typically carried out by governmental actors that aim to increase their political power and may include various tools such as (packed) courts, constitutional amendments, excessive litigation, or partisan legal interpretations.

We also advance '**state lawfare**' as an important subdivision of domestic lawfare used in internal territorial conflicts. Internal territorial conflicts often take place against a backdrop of divided loyalties and competing politico-legal systems where two polities lay claim to the same territory, as in the case of secessionist movements. States of exception, special orders, incarceration of political and civil society leaders, and temporary loss of civil liberties are all key elements of how governments employ state lawfare to 'solve' disputes with minority territorial groups. While this can be brutally effective in the short run, it may weaken the possibility for long-term settlements due to furthering grievances between political opponents.

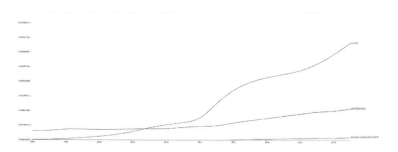

Figure 1.2 Lawfare's appearances in printed sources (2000–2019)
Source: Google Books Ngram Viewer, 2022; Michel *et al.*, 2011

The last type of lawfare in our conceptualisation is '**asymmetric lawfare**'. Although lawfare is perhaps generally associated with powerful actors, particularly states, both small, 'weak' states and non-state actors such as civil society groups also resort to lawfare for a range of politically driven purposes. This includes litigation against larger, more powerful states or transnational companies, both in national and international courts.

As will be elaborated throughout the book, the different dimensions of lawfare have an element in common; they involve conflictual dynamics between political actors and typically occur in the context of deeply asymmetrical power relationships. Perhaps these elements help to explain why lawfare has crossed the border from academia to mainstream society, becoming a popular term in contemporary political debates across the globe. This is partly evidenced by the sharp increase in appearances of lawfare in printed sources. As Figure 1.2 illustrates, the term has, in recent years, surpassed in popularity similar concepts such as 'judicialisation' and 'abusive constitutionalism'. In effect, in recent years, there has been a proliferation of cases where journalists, policymakers, and activists in various geographic areas have used the term lawfare to refer to what we term *domestic lawfare*. In these cases, lawfare has clear negative connotations as it refers to situations in which the law is weaponised to de-legitimise and fight internal adversaries (Zanin *et al.*, 2021).

Our book uses a blended method combining theoretical conceptualisations with real life examples of the various dimensions of lawfare, using a wide range of case studies that span the globe across four different continents. This geographic diversity shows that lawfare is indeed a global phenomenon. The book chapters are organised according to the four dimensions of lawfare outlined earlier: geopolitical lawfare, domestic lawfare, state lawfare, and asymmetric lawfare.

Chapter 2 focuses on the traditional understanding of the term as 'the use of law as a weapon of war'. We argue that geopolitical lawfare is one of the instruments in the panoply of measures that states have at their disposal to consolidate their power in the international arena. The chapter scrutinises the geopolitical uses of lawfare by analysing the lawfare strategies – and implementations – of the US, the People's Republic of China, and the Russian Federation. This chapter concludes that typically geopolitical lawfare is not used *instead of* but *in conjunction with* other instruments.

Chapter 3 critically examines domestic lawfare, involving power accumulation and the (ab)use of state legal instruments to undermine political adversaries. We argue that in authoritarian regimes, domestic lawfare is inherent to the system. Conversely, in liberal democratic regimes, it is an anomalous practice that has potentially damaging consequences. To illustrate our argument, we use examples of democratic polities in Europe and Latin America, where domestic lawfare erodes judicial independence and, in the most severe cases, leads to the incarceration of opposition figures.

Building on the insights from Chapter 3, Chapter 4 illustrates the use of state lawfare in internal territorial conflicts. It analyses, for example, the use of state lawfare in historical cases such as the territorial dispossession of Native Americans in the United States. It also examines more contemporary applications of state lawfare in territorial conflicts such as Northern Ireland, the Basque Country, and Catalonia. This chapter shows that while state lawfare can be an effective instrument for central governments in territorial domestic conflicts, it has potentially significant drawbacks for the long-term solution of grievances and can even harm fundamental liberal rights in democratic systems.

Subsequently, Chapter 5 highlights that lawfare can also be an instrument used by disempowered actors, such as civil society organisations, to legally challenge states or transnational companies. The chapter illustrates this argument with examples that combine environmental lawfare and human rights litigation, such as in the Ogoni case in Nigeria and the Dakota Access Pipeline protest movement on the Standing Rock Indian Reservation. We also show how small states or sub-state actors attempt to resist stronger adversaries through a strategy of counter-lawfare such as Nicaragua, Ukraine, or Palestine. While the use of asymmetric lawfare may provide some leverage and even symbolic victories for 'weak' actors, the structural hierarchies inherent to political conflict tend to favour the stronger parties in the end.

Finally, Chapter 6 concludes the book with a succinct summary, emphasising the importance of understanding lawfare as a multifaceted instrument of power that involves different types of cases and multiple actors, both as perpetrators as well as victims of it. It also speculates about the future of lawfare as a concept.

Chapter 2

Geopolitical lawfare

Legal instruments as weapons of war

2.1 Introduction

In the wake of September 11, during the so-called war on terror, former US Major General Charles Dunlap reframed – and popularised –
the term lawfare. Dunlap's popular interpretation has had profound
conceptual consequences for lawfare, making the international geopolitical aspect the hegemonic understanding of the term, at least in
academia. This is illustrated, for example, by the abundant body of
literature that overwhelmingly focuses on this particular dimension
while ignoring other aspects of lawfare. In line with our new conceptualisation, we understand this particular dimension of the term as
'geopolitical lawfare'.

Interestingly, while Dunlap's definition was admittedly inspired by
Carlson and Yeomans' initial coining (1975), he provided the concept
with a remarkably different meaning, situating it within the international military-security domain and describing it as 'a method of warfare where law is used as a means of realizing a military objective'
(2001: 4). A few years later, Dunlap refined his reconceptualisation
with the broadly popular and widely cited definition of lawfare as 'the
strategy of using – or misusing – law as a substitute for traditional military means to achieve an operational objective' (Dunlap, 2008: 146).
This narrow definition fits well with the perception of lawfare as 'legal
warfare' but does not encapsulate the other facets of lawfare, which we
will analyse in subsequent chapters.

Dunlap's definition entails turning upside down Clausewitz's famous
conception of war as a continuation of politics by other means (1984:
87). Reversely, it has Foucauldian (Foucault, 2003: 15)[1] underpinnings
as lawfare is seen as 'a continuation of war by legal means' (Morrissey,
2011: 291). Kennedy illustrates this seemingly symbiotic relationship

DOI: 10.4324/9781003289869-2

between law and war with an imperfect chiasmus, '[W]e make war in the shadow of law, and law in the shadow of force' (2006: 167). Following Dunlap's reinterpretation, scholars in law and international relations have overwhelmingly understood lawfare as 'the use of law as a weapon of war' (Kennedy, 2006; Weizman, 2010; Trachtman, 2016; Cai, 2019).

Kennedy, for instance, concisely defined lawfare as 'the waging of war by law' (2006: 12). In a similar vein, Austin and Kolenc have conceptualised lawfare as 'exploiting judicial processes to achieve political or military objectives' (2006: 1). The underlying idea of this understanding, based on the exploitation of international law instruments, is that lawfare is closely linked to hybrid warfare and asymmetric warfare (Newton, 2010, Weizman, 2010; Trachtman, 2016; Munoz Mosquera *et al.*, 2019). In fact, some go as far as to claim that it plays a central role in hybrid warfare (Munoz Mosquera and Bachmann, 2016: 87).

Here, a clarification needs to be made in relation to whether lawfare is a soft power instrument or otherwise. While some have conceived it as 'soft power geopolitics' (Falk, 2015), we dispute this categorisation by virtue of the definition of soft power coined by the 'father' of the term, Joseph Nye. This influential international relations (IR) scholar defined it as 'the ability to obtain preferred outcomes through attraction', distinguishing it from hard power instruments which were characterised by 'the use of coercion' (1990: 160). In our perspective, although lawfare could be seen as an *in-between*, it is closer to being a hard power mechanism based on 'coercion' than a soft power one based on 'attraction'. At any rate, lawfare belongs to the all-encompassing strategy of smart power, which Nye describes as the 'ability to combine hard and soft power into successful strategies where they reinforce rather than contradict each other' (2021: 2–3).

We note that, unlike other types of lawfare which will be analysed in subsequent chapters, Dunlap's understanding of lawfare is exclusively located in the international arena and is primarily utilised by state actors in their pursuit of foreign policy aims. This chapter will consequently focus on interactions between state actors that use legal instruments in international contexts characterised by (endemic) security competition and antagonistic interests.[2] As such, this dimension is particularly appealing for great powers – or states with an ambitious interventionist foreign policy – as it allows them to increase their relative power and accomplish multiple political objectives.

Seen from this realist perspective, lawfare is *just* another instrument among the panoply of measures that states have at their disposal to strengthen their position in the international system. As some of our examples will show next, lawfare is neither exclusive nor used isolatedly. That is very often it is not used *instead of* but *in conjunction* or *in coordination with* other instruments. Perhaps one of the key differences between lawfare and purely military operations is that the former is significantly less costly, both regarding financial expenses and in terms of human casualties.

2.2 Why is geopolitical lawfare a popular tool?

The explanation for the popularity of the new conceptualisation is multifaceted, containing utilitarian and institutional elements. To begin with, given that legal matters have become ubiquitous in military conflicts (Werner, 2010: 66) and are 'a fact of modern war' (Dunlap, 2008: 149), it makes sense that there is a concept describing this phenomenon. Simply put, it is useful to have a short, concise, and *catchy* term that encompasses this particular reality. Arguably, the term also derives its strength from the suffix 'fare' (coming from 'warfare'), which reflects an inherent conflictual dynamic, making it more attractive for practitioners, scholars, and international affairs pundits alike.

As explained previously, in utilitarian terms, lawfare offers a wide range of advantages compared to traditional hard power instruments, not least the fact that it can be more effective (Kittrie, 2016). First and foremost, it reduces destructiveness and mortality, or at least, the visibility of casualties.[3] As Goldenziel graphically puts it, lawfare is a 'potent weapon that leaves fewer bodies on the battlefield' (2020: 1171). The example of the MV Alaed, a Russian cargo ship allegedly carrying weapons destined to the Syrian government at the early stages of the war in the Levantine country, has been used to illustrate this point (Kittrie, 2016: 2). Under pressure from Washington and London, the cargo's insurers (Standard Club) were compelled to withdraw the ship's insurance, effectively forcing the ship to return to Russia (Black and Carrell, 2012). This lawfare tactic provided, at low economic cost and without risking any major confrontation, a strategic victory for the US and the UK, who prevented a weapon shipment destined to what they perceived as a rogue state through purely legal means.

In addition to these utilitarian factors, Cai (2019) points out that there are reasons of a more institutional and systemic nature: namely, the increasing importance of international law as a regulator of the legality (and legitimacy) of international relations. This idea is somewhat connected to the Kelsenian notion of the primacy of international law, as 'the highest sovereign legal order' (1967: 217), standing above national legal orders. This subordination of states to international law has, following Kelsen's logic, crucial consequences for the international order. Kelsen, similar to Kant (1795/1917) a century and a half earlier, idealistically envisioned that international peace could be achieved through global institutions and international law:

> When the question arises how to secure international peace, how to eliminate the most terrible employment of force – namely, war – from inter-State relations, no answer seems to be more self evident than this: to unite all individual states, or at least, as many as possible, into a World State, to concentrate all their means of power, their armed forces, and put them at the disposal of a world government under laws created by a world parliament.
>
> (Kelsen, 1944/2000: 4–5)

Kelsen's legal idealism which presupposes that 'a durable peace' can be achieved 'within the framework of international law' (1944/2000: 12) is, unsurprisingly, overtly disputed by IR realist theorists. The influential realist scholar, Hans Morgenthau, for instance, was more than sceptical with the premise regarding the importance of international law and its ability to peacefully settle international disputes. Morgenthau concluded in unambiguous terms that 'what really mattered in relations among nations was not international law but international politics' (1978: 65). Similarly, Edward Carr argues that international law is 'more frankly political than other branches of law' and, consequently, in this type of law is where 'the power element is more predominant' (Carr, 1939/2016: 165).

Reversing Kelsen's argument 180 degrees, Morgenthau, Carr, and realists in general view the relationship between international law and politics as asymmetrical, yet with the former being inevitably subordinated to the latter. This subordination has vital consequences for lawfare as it partly explains its emergence – and importance – in contemporary international conflicts. In Morgenthau's perspective, international law does not replace power politics but channels it (1951), representing a useful tool that allows states to consolidate their power or *national interest* (1948/2005). According to the realist interpretation, international law is primarily viewed as a 'resource' instrumentalised by states (Hurd, 2011: 294).

The practice of lawfare, in the previously mentioned understanding as the instrumentalisation of legal instruments to pursue operational and geopolitical objectives, is palpably more in line with cynical views of international law than with idealist interpretations. While the practice can on some occasions solve conflicts, 'international law can also cause or exacerbate' them (Pogies, 2021: 144). This is particularly the case when the law becomes a 'meaningful weapon' to defend and enforce state interests (Cai, 2019: 272), like it occurs with the use (and abuse) of lawfare instruments.

Let us now turn our attention to the specific cases of how great powers use legal instruments to further their national interests in the international arena.

2.3 Great powers' attitudes and strategies towards geopolitical lawfare

Some of the academic discussions on lawfare have been centred around the normative question of how to judge the concept from a moral standpoint. While Dunlap admitted that the practice can be used 'for good or bad purposes' (2008: 146), at a later stage he concluded that 'on balance – lawfare in its many forms has been much more of a positive force than a negative one' (2010: 142). Conversely, for others, lawfare 'always has a negative connotation as a phenomenon that denies the law' (Zanin et al., 2021: 8). It must be noted, however, that the aforementioned authors refer here not to geopolitical lawfare but to what we describe as 'state lawfare' (see Chapter 3).

Dunlap claims that lawfare (at least in its geopolitical form) is 'ideologically neutral' (2017: 9). Multiple scholars agree with the argument that lawfare as an analytical concept is neutral (Newton, 2010; Kittrie, 2016; Gloppen, 2018). However, this conceptual neutrality does not preclude the possibility of using the instrument to pursue a particular political objective or national interest. For us, the most pertinent aspect of the alleged neutrality of lawfare is that, like other power instruments such as military technology, unmanned aerial vehicles (UAVs), or soft power tools, it can be used by a wide range of actors to accomplish various political objectives.

The key idea is that no actor has the monopoly of this instrument; its use will depend on political will and the (legal) capabilities of a given state. In that sense, lawfare is, indeed, 'neutral'. This section offers a succinct glimpse of the strategic use of geopolitical lawfare of the three great powers – the US, the People's Republic of China (PRC), and the Russian Federation – with the mightiest military capabilities in the world (see GlobalFirePower, 2022).

2.3.1 The US vis-à-vis geopolitical lawfare

One of Dunlap's primary purposes is to scrutinise to what extent lawfare may undercut the ability of the US to conduct effective military interventions (2008, 2009, 2017). Indeed, Dunlap envisions geopolitical lawfare as a tool to advance the national and military interests of the US, as illustrated by the conclusion of one of his most reputable articles: '[T]oday more than ever our nation needs the synergistic efforts of the entire government, both military and civilian, to succeed in today's complex lawfare milieu' (Dunlap, 2008: 149). A specific example mentioned by Dunlap consists of 'legal preparation of the battlespace' training so that troops, and particularly US army commanders, gain familiarisation with the laws of war (and lawfare) and incorporate them in their planning and operational processes (Dunlap, 2017: 12).

Dunlap is not alone in advocating for more US engagement with this instrument. Various scholars and think-tankers claim that Western states, and particularly the US, should start recognising the strategic value of law as a military doctrine (Sari, 2020). Goldenziel puts it bluntly by arguing that 'the US must develop a lawfare strategy' on the grounds that such a strategy would 'improve whole-of government efforts to combat our adversaries using law' (2020: 1171). In the same vein, Kittrie does not conceal his frustration at the fact that the US 'has no lawfare strategy or doctrine', which he deems as 'a tremendous missed opportunity' (2016: 3).

As we shall explain later, Kittrie's disappointment is not entirely justified, given Washington's substantial use of this instrument as a foreign policy tool. The absence of an institutionalised lawfare doctrine is, however, visible in the National Security Strategies of the United States (White House, 2017, 2021[4]), where lawfare shines by its absence. Beyond some vague references to the importance of 'the rule of law', there is no formulation of a specific strategy[5] regarding law in the international arena, as there is with other 'pillars' such as military might, cyberspace, diplomacy, or values (White House, 2017).

While the US does not have a specific strategic framework on lawfare, it recurrently does resort to it as a *tactic* to deal with foreign policy challenges. Lawfare, in other words, is used by the US more in practice, or *ad hoc*, than in theory as a foreign policy instrument in numerous war – and hybrid war – contexts. As the section 'Geopolitical lawfare methods in the international arena' will explore in great detail, the US has used and abused a wide range of lawfare tools in recent years, including international sanctions, lawfare through international organisations as well as discursive lawfare. Sanctions – the US' preferred lawfare method in the past decades – have been broadly employed as a first resort by successive (Obama, Trump, and Biden) administrations to deal with a wide range of policy challenges (Drezner, 2021). As we will show later, the US uses this legally enforced instrument against state actors and organisations (such as companies) but also against individual persons.[6] There are abundant examples of recent US financial warfare targeting geopolitical foes with sanctions, including the PRC (e.g. US Department of Treasury, 2022a), the Islamic Republic of Iran (e.g. White House, 2019), Cuba (where a quasi-total embargo has been in place since 1962), and the Russian Federation (e.g. US Department of Treasury, 2022b).

Lawfare, Dunlap warns, can also be exploited as a strategy by the 'enemies' of the United States with the aim of challenging its military operations and therefore its military might (Dunlap, 2001, 2007, 2017). It is important to emphasise that while Dunlap's primary focus is on the actual – and potential – use of this instrument by the US, this great power does not have a monopoly on or exclusive rights over geopolitical lawfare. To further articulate this argument, the following paragraphs will shed light on the perspective of lawfare by the geopolitical adversaries of the United States.

2.3.2 Lawfare and the People's Republic of China

It is no secret that the PRC is, as of 2022, a great power with potential to replace the United States as a global hegemon or, at least, to significantly challenge the primacy that the latter has enjoyed since the end of the Cold War. Some have suggested the possibility of a new bipolar order 'in which the US – China rivalry' could affect 'virtually every aspect of international politics' (Zhao, 2022: 169). One of these aspects is lawfare, which is viewed by the Chinese leadership as an instrument that can boost the 'political initiative' and lead to 'military victory' (Lee, 2014: 203).

In a famous speech delivered in 1996 at a Chinese Communist Party (CCP) Central Committee seminar, Chinese President at the time Jiang Zemin stated that '[W]e must be adept at using international law as "a weapon" to defend the interests of our state' (cited by Wang, 2005: 128). As the readers may have noticed, this sentence perfectly epitomises Morgenthau's instrumental perspective of international law previously outlined. Three years after President Zemin's speech, in 1999, the influential military strategy book 'Unrestricted Warfare', written by two People's Liberation Army[7] (PLA) colonels, was published. The manuscript represents a paradigm shift in the sense that it challenges the orthodox view that armed forces are the only instrument able to 'compel the enemy to submit to one's will', replacing it with the premise that 'all means, including . . . military and non-military, and lethal and non-lethal means' must be used 'to compel the enemy to accept one's interests' (Qiao and Wang, 1999: 7). It did not take long for lawfare, or as the authors put it 'international law warfare' (ibid.: 55), to be incorporated into the PRC's military strategy.

The legal codification of legal warfare as part of the PRC's strategic doctrine finally materialised when a document drafted by the PLA, the 'Political Work Regulations', was eventually promulgated by the CCP in 2003 (Cheng, 2012; Lee, 2014). This document develops a three-fold strategy, the 'Three Warfares', combining soft and hard power tools which encompass three hybrid warfare areas: media/public opinion, psychology, and legal warfare (US Department of Defense, 2021). The latter's main rationale is summarised in simple terms by Yanrong as follows: 'arguing that one's own side is obeying the law' while simultaneously 'criticizing the other side for violating the law [weifa]' (cited by Cheng, 2012: 2). More comprehensively, a 2007 PLA official textbook characterised lawfare as the use of law as a 'weapon' through a wide range of methods, such as 'legal deterrence, legal attack, legal counterattack, legal restraint, legal sanctions, and legal protections' (cited by Odom, 2011: 224).

It seems therefore clear that the PRC has a much more developed strategy, at least formally, regarding lawfare than the US. Whereas Washington uses it extensively on a tactical level, lawfare is fully embedded in the PRC's strategic doctrine. In recent years, the codification of legal welfare tools has become more prominent as evidenced, for example, by the 2020 National Defense Law. The Pentagon, with a considerable degree of concern, believes that such law 'broadened the legal justification for PLA mobilization to include defense of China's economic interests' with the aim of increasing the 'legitimacy to the use of military force to defend the PRC's economic interests abroad' (US Department of Defense, 2021: 3).

With this context in mind, it becomes essential to succinctly analyse specific lawfare-oriented policies pursued by the PRC. The South China Sea[8] (SCS), a quintessential faultline in contemporary geopolitics, provides a splendid illustration of the intersection between lawfare, economic interests, military build-ups, and multilateral tensions coupled with competing territorial claims. Predictably, the use of lawfare in the fascinating SCS quagmire has reinvigorated the academic interest towards lawfare, attracting the attention of a significant number of academic studies which, in turn, have contributed to revisit the concept (Odom, 2011; Hong, 2012; Guilfoyle, 2019; Goldenziel, 2020; Pogies, 2021).

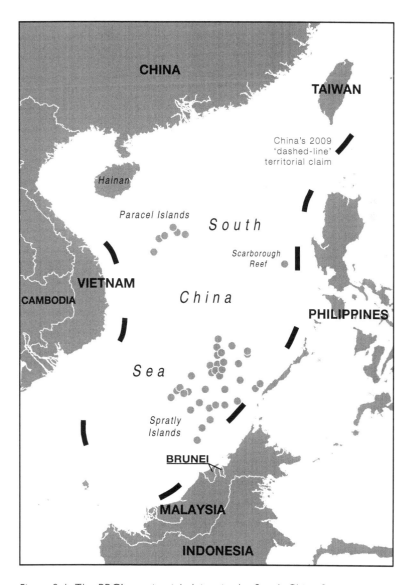

Figure 2.1 The PRC's territorial claims in the South China Sea

Source: elaborated by Steven M. Radil, 2022

As Guilfoyle claims, 'law is a key domain through which it [the PRC] seeks to consolidate control over the South China Sea' (2019: 999). Lawfare is useful in this area for a plethora of reasons. First, it allows states, not just the PRC, to establish sovereignty claims over disputed islands and archipelagos. This is done, for example, through the UN Convention on the Law of the Sea (UNCLOS), an international agreement signed in 1982 that aims to settle 'all issues relating to the law of the sea' (United Nations, 1982: 25), including the pivotal matter of 'sovereignty over the territorial sea' (ibid.: 27).

The problem for the PRC is that, as explained earlier, no state has exclusive rights when it comes to using legal instruments or, indeed, lawfare. According to Goldenziel, the Philippines's decision, supported and encouraged by the US, to institute arbitral proceedings (under UNCLOS) through the Permanent Court of Arbitration (PCA), in 2013, constitutes a clear-cut case of lawfare: '[U]nable to confront China militarily on its own over these violations of its sovereignty, the Philippines turned to instrumental lawfare to achieve a military objective' (2020: 1085). Beijing experienced a resounding legal defeat when the PCA eventually ruled, in 2016, that 'there was no legal basis for China to claim historic rights[9]' (Permanent Court of Arbitration, 2016: 2) in the contested maritime area.

According to Pogies, all states formulating maritime and territorial claims construct them 'as legal claims and not as claims based on mere economic or military power' (2021: 145). The PRC's claim over various islands in the SCS such as the Spratly Islands[10] is justified by the Chinese government's argument, reproduced in various official statements, that Chinese sovereignty over these territories has solid 'legal grounds' (Chinese Ministry of Foreign Affairs, 2020) and is 'consistent with international law' (United Nations, 2020a: 1). Conversely, China's geopolitical adversaries such as Australia, use similar fora and similar legal parlance such as '[T]here is no legal basis for a maritime feature to generate maritime entitlements' (United Nations, 2020b: 1–2) to refute Beijing's claims. Similarly, the US Department of State recurrently uses the argument that China's sovereignty claims in the SCS are 'unlawful' (2022).

Second, such legal claims (and its refutations) have enormous potential military consequences. In the particular context of the SCS, given the geostrategic importance of the area, lawfare-oriented actions pursued by the PRC are aimed *inter alia* at challenging US military presence in the area. In this area, legal claims have not just been used on paper but have also played a key role in connection to specific serious incidents between two nuclear superpowers. For example, on numerous occasions in 2021, the Chinese government issued formal complaints about alleged legal violations carried out by US military ships. Following what the PRC viewed as US vessels trespassing into Chinese territorial waters, PLA spokesperson, Tian Junli, stated that the US had 'seriously violated China's sovereignty and security . . . international laws and basic principles in international relations' (cited by Zhihao, 2021). The US typically frames its response to these allegations using lawfare parameters. In September 2021, after a maritime incident in the SCS involving a US destroyer, the US Navy issued a statement defending the lawfulness of their operation, claiming that its ship 'conducted this FONOP [Freedom of Navigation Operation] in accordance with international law. . ...The operation reflects our commitment to uphold freedom of navigation and lawful uses of the sea as a principle' (US Navy, 2021).

Third, it is not too far-fetched to argue that the goal of using lawfare, both in theory and in praxis, in this area is to alter the regional – and conceivably global – balance of power. That being said, the US and PRC lawfare in the SCS does not happen *in vacuo* but in conjunction with political assertiveness and, most importantly, in a context of increasing military presence by both global powers.

2.3.3 The Russian Federation and lawfare

The Russian Federation is no stranger to lawfare (Bartman, 2010; Dunlap, 2017; Goldenziel, 2020; Tropin, 2021). In unambiguous terms, Dunlap affirms that lawfare is a part of 'Russia's arsenal', specifically, an essential element of Moscow's 'hybrid war' strategy (2017: 12). Bartman provides a historical perspective by arguing that lawfare in contemporary Russia is directly *inherited* from its predecessor state, the Soviet Union, which profusely used it as 'a supplement to military strategy . . . with a strategic intent and political motivation to manipulate the legal system, international bodies and other states' (2010: 428).

In contemporary Russia, lawfare is, in effect, present in its strategic documents. For instance, in its National Security Strategy, legal instruments are explicitly recognised as one of the measures that Russia can use to deal with 'threats to national security' (Kremlin, 2021: 2). Russia's Foreign Policy Concept provides a much more elaborated and detailed picture of the potential uses of lawfare. This strategic document mentions the fact that, like the PRC, Moscow can use legal instruments 'to delimitate the state boundary of the Russian Federation as well as its maritime boundaries' (Russian Ministry of Foreign Affairs, 2016). The additional references to lawfare instruments are all connected to countering US policies, leverage, and global hegemony. For instance, the strategic document advocates for the use of international legal instruments 'to prevent military interventions . . . under the pretext of implementing the "responsibility to protect" concept' and to avert 'the US policy of extraterritorial jurisdiction[11] beyond the boundaries of international law' (Russian Ministry of Foreign Affairs, 2016).

At the core of Russian lawfare, therefore, we find what Allison refers to as 'the normative basis of international order', that is, a legal-based challenge 'over who makes the rules and how such rules are applied' (2013: 170). Russia's engagement with normative lawfare to criticise Western interventions is arguably less connected to a genuine belief in legal orthodoxy and more to the foreign policy purpose of 'enmeshing the western liberal democracies in a web of legal and normative constraints' (Averre and Davies, 2015: 827). These legal critiques have been used to lambast the US – and NATO – for their illegal, that is unauthorised by the UNSC, military interventions in Yugoslavia (1999), Iraq (2003), and to a certain extent, Libya (2011). The latter was sanctioned by UNSC resolution 1973 (United Nations, 2011), but according to the Russian Federation, NATO abused the UN mandate by using the pretext of protecting civilians to conduct a classic regime change operation. As Russia's Foreign Minister, Sergei Lavrov, put it, less than a month after NATO initiated its *Unified Protector* mission, '[T]he UN Security Council never aimed to topple the Libyan regime. All those who are currently using the UN resolution for that aim are violating the UN mandate' (cited by Al Jazeera, 2011).

Lawfare is not only employed passively to highlight illegalities by Western powers, but it has also been used in the context of military – or hybrid – operations conducted by the Russian Federation. This more proactive type of lawfare plays a lesser role in strategic documents. Following the March 2014 annexation[12] of Crimea, the use of lawfare strategies became more prominent. In his celebratory speech to the Duma, the President of the Russian Federation, Vladimir V. Putin, explicitly referred to the 'Kosovo precedent' and the 2010 International Court of Justice's (ICJ) *advisory opinion*[13] (Kremlin, 2014) to justify the legality of the Peninsula's annexation. This reference could be interpreted as Moscow's political vendetta, in the sense that if legal principles such as territorial integrity 'could be compromised by the West [in Kosovo] with impunity, these very norms can also be twisted by Russia in the name of "protection of civilians" and national interest' (Castan Pinos, 2019: 167).

Figure 2.2 Map of Ukraine

Source: United Nations, 2014

Russia's territorial and military control of Crimea has not been a mere border transformation: it has led to fundamental geopolitical consequences in the region. Chief among them, the fact that Moscow gained exclusive control over the Strait of Kerch, thus being able to control the shipping flows between the Black Sea and the Sea of Azov, with the potential to trap the Ukrainian Navy in the latter. Åtland contends that Crimea's annexation coupled with expanded military presence in the northern Black Sea has allowed Russia 'to unilaterally redraw the maritime borders . . . and redefine the region's political and legal orders' (2021: 319). The Russian invasion of Ukraine in February 2022 can be considered an expansion of Russia's unilateral – and illegal – strategy of redrawing its neighbours' borders while attempting to impose its political will through brute force.

One particular incident clearly illustrates this dynamic as well as the proactive use of Russian lawfare. In November 2018, the Russian

Federal Security Service (FSB) border patrol forcibly seized three Ukrainian Navy vessels in the Strait of Kerch, alleging that they had illegally entered Russian territorial waters (France 24, 2018). The diplomatic services of both states subsequently engaged in a war of words, where they emphasised the legality of their respective actions and denounced the illegality of the actions conducted by their adversaries (Russian Ministry of Foreign Affairs, 2018; Ukrainian Ministry of Foreign Affairs, 2018). This incident illustrates, once again, the fact that lawfare is not used *in vacuo* but in strategic coordination with other instruments of power.

Last but certainly not least, we briefly discuss an instrument that Russia has recurrently used in various conflicts in recent years: private military companies (PMCs). Kevin Rousseau argues that the use of PMCs constitutes a clear case of lawfare, being particularly useful in hybrid warfare contexts (2017). One of the key problems with these actors is the lack of 'an effective system of national and international law to govern their use' (Pattison, 2014: 4), which often leads to an 'accountability vacuum' (Mackinnon, 2021). Paradoxically, this *problem* is precisely one of the main reasons that accounts for the popularity of PMCs not only for Russia, but also for the US – as illustrated by Washington's security reliance on the controversial 'Blackwater' PMC during the war in Iraq – and other great powers. The lack of accountability allows states to go the *extra mile*, circumventing legal boundaries and constraints via such proxy troops.

In the case of Russia, the Wagner Group deserves special attention. Various authors highlight the salient contradiction that while this PMC is not officially legal in Russia, Moscow has used its security-military services on multiple occasions (Marten, 2019; Østensen and Bukkvoll, 2022) in foreign military operations such as in Donbass, Eastern Ukraine, and Syria (Wagner Group,[14] 2022). The former is a particularly relevant case regarding lawfare. Not least because, until the Russian invasion of Ukraine in February 2022, the use of the Wagner Group and other PMCs have allowed Russia to (indirectly) intervene in the conflict while maintaining plausible deniability, that is, denying direct military involvement (Østensen and Bukkvoll, 2022). This perfectly illustrates the attractiveness of PMCs for the Russian Federation and for any other state, for that matter. The use of PMCs allows them to outsource – and to a certain extent conceal – controversial military engagements that are legally contentious and potentially unpopular, without compromising the operational objectives.

2.4 Geopolitical lawfare methods in the international arena

After briefly explaining the strategic use – and importance – of lawfare for three great powers, this section will explore in-depth various lawfare tools that states employ to pursue their national interests. By doing so, this final section inverts the telescope, vis-à-vis the previous, to put the focus not on agents of lawfare but on specific lawfare methods. This exploration will serve the purpose of deepening our conceptualisation of the international security dimension of lawfare. Due to space constraints, it will not be possible to examine *all* types of lawfare tactics (cf. Kittrie, 2016). Instead, we will concentrate on three methods (sanctions, lawfare through international organisations, and rhetoric) that have had a pervasive significance in recent years. Interestingly, some of these tools do not necessarily appear connected to lawfare at first glance. For example, the instrument we examine next: sanctions.

2.4.1 Sanctions

Sanctions were conceptualised by Kelsen as a punitive mechanism 'established by international law' against a state based on the principles of 'collective liability of the members of the state for the international delicts committed by the government' (1967: 324–325). More recently, Nephew has defined sanctions as a 'constellation of laws, authorities, and obligations laid out in a piece of legislation, government decree, UN resolution ... that restrict or prohibit what is normally permissible conduct' (2017: 8). Both definitions point in the same direction: sanctions are closely intertwined with lawfare. Indeed, while sanctions are instruments often associated with coercive economics (Drezner, 2021) or geoeconomics, various scholars argue that this policy should also be considered lawfare (Dunlap, 2009, 2010; Kittrie, 2016; Chifu, 2017) as their operability directly relies on legal coercive means to ensure compliance.

It is important to note that while its popularity has surged in the 21st century, this legally enforced mechanism of collective punishment is not an entirely contemporary phenomenon. The practice gained critical relevance in the aftermath of WWI, when sanctions were legally codified in article 16 of the Covenant[15] of the League of Nations. The League used the mechanism on four occasions, the most renowned being the sanctions against fascist Italy (1935–1936), which failed due to lack of compliance by several European states (Baer, 1973; Davis and Engerman, 2003). Like the League, the United Nations codified international sanctions in its foundational treaty, the UN Charter (1945). The latter, however, has used this mechanism through its Security Council (the UNSC) much more frequently (particularly since the 1990s), more prominently, and in innovative ways that were 'surely never dreamed by those who framed the UN Charter at San Francisco' (Gowlland-Debbas, 2021: 1).

The coercive nature of sanctions cannot be overlooked. Indeed, this mechanism is intended to alter the targeted state's behaviour through the infliction of 'notable cost' in the form of hardship and pain, which more often than not is endured by civilians (Weiss, 1999; Pattison, 2018). The fact that civilians, not the targeted elites, are the main victims of sanctions constitutes in itself a critique against this instrument. The amorality of sanctions is perhaps best epitomised by the infamous quote (for which she apologised *a fortiori*) by former US Secretary of State, Madeleine Albright, who stated that the death of half a million Iraqi children as a result of the UNSC imposed sanctions (see later section) was a price 'worth' paying to undermine Saddam Hussein's rule (CBS, 1996). On the other hand, sanctions are justified on the grounds that they are a 'lesser evil' between war and inaction, and because they may be effective, for instance, in having a positive impact regarding human rights (Pattison, 2018: 69). In line with his well-known idealism, back in 1919, US President Woodrow Wilson envisioned sanctions as a 'peaceful' and reasonable alternative to war (1919: 23).

At this stage, two critical questions arise: what kind of sanctions can be imposed, and which actors implement them? Sanctions can target a wide range of issues. Nephew identifies four main types: diplomatic, economic, technological, and military (2017: 44–48). These different types are not exclusive, as different types may be imposed simultaneously. Drezner offers a useful insight into economic sanctions by distinguishing between trade sanctions, historically more popular yet less efficient as they may be evaded through trade in the black market, and a newer and *smarter* subtype: financial sanctions (2015). The latter gives extraordinary influence to the US given the Western dominance over the international financial system (Arnold, 2016; Nephew, 2017).

As for which actors use the mechanism of sanctions, it basically boils down to two: states and intergovernmental organisations. The latter are commonly known as multilateral sanctions and are imposed, for instance, within the UN Security Council framework. The prohibition of all imports of commodities and goods from Iraq following the invasion of Kuwait in 1990 (United Nations, 1990: 19) constitutes an archetypical example of multilateral sanctions issued by this UN body.

However, this case also illustrates a fundamental limitation of sanctions. Despite the draconian nature of these sanctions, which led to the collapse of Iraq's economy and a dramatic increase in infant mortality, the Iraqi government did not withdraw from Kuwait nor comply with any other of the UNSC's demands (Drezner, 1999).

On the other hand, states may also impose sanctions more unilaterally. In principle, any powerful state may resort to sanctions; the US, however, clearly outshines the rest. So much so that various authors concur that this lawfare-based instrument has become Washington's favourite foreign policy tool (Drezner, 2015, 2021; Nephew, 2017; Terry, 2019). This is particularly visible when it comes to financial sanctions, where the US is considered an 'undisputed ... hegemon' (Drezner, 2015: 758). One of the architects of this policy, former Assistant Secretary of the US Treasury Juan Zárate, describes the rationale of what he defines as 'financial warfare' in the following terms: '[W]e viewed the global battlefield through the lens of dollars, euros, and rials, seeing money as our greatest asset and our enemies' greatest vulnerability' (2013: 2).

As seen earlier, numerous states – including great powers such as the PRC and the Russian Federation – have been a target of the so-called US' financial warfare. The most recent example illustrating the pre-eminence of this policy is the barrel of sanctions imposed against Russia following Moscow's invasion of Ukraine in February 2022. The most important US response to said invasion was the imposition – in coordination with its European allies – of 'severe' and 'unprecedented' sanctions against the Russian Federation aimed at entirely isolating its economy 'from international finance and commerce' (US Department of Treasury, 2022c). The 2022 wave of sanctions effectively meant that Russia became the most sanctioned state in the world, overcoming Iran, Syria, and North Korea (Castellum.AI, 2022).

The sanction regime designed and imposed by Washington has a controversial wrinkle which specifically relates to lawfare due to its secondary and extraterritorial nature. That is, whereas primary sanctions legally prohibit US individuals and companies from doing business with a state targeted by US sanctions, secondary sanctions are aimed at non-US citizens and entities, which can be legally prosecuted for, basically, not following US foreign policy directives. Critics argue that secondary, or extraterritorial, US sanctions simultaneously violate customary international law and state sovereignty:

> by attempting to compel non-resident foreign companies and foreign citizens to comply with US sanction laws even when acting

outside of the US, the US is implicitly trying to compel them to undermine their home State's foreign policy if it is not aligned with US foreign policy.

(Terry, 2019: 427)

Interestingly, the extraterritorial coerciveness of secondary sanctions directly affects the US' closest allies. One of the main EU foreign policy agencies, the Institute for Security Studies, has labelled the US sanction regime as a 'geopolitical challenge' for the EU, because it compels (and punishes) EU companies 'even though these restrictions are not embraced by the EU', thus jeopardising the bloc's cherished 'strategic autonomy' (Portela, 2021: 2). In the same vein, former German Minister of Foreign Affairs Heiko Maas expressed in an unusually harsh tone his opposition to potential US sanctions against European companies engaged in the Nord Stream 2 project: '[B]y announcing measures that will also sanction European companies, the US government is disregarding the right and sovereignty of Europe.... European energy policy is made in Europe and not in Washington. We clearly reject extraterritorial sanctions' (Maas cited by China Daily, 2020).

Finally, we will focus on a particular case that patently illustrates the concomitance between (secondary) economic sanctions and lawfare. In December 2018, Wanzhou Meng, the CFO of Chinese tech giant Huawei, was arrested in Canada at the request of US authorities on charges of fraud (BBC, 2018). However, this was not an ordinary case of fraud. According to the US indictment, Meng[16] had served on the board of a Huawei subsidiary company (Skycom) that had 'conducted its business in Iran in a manner that violated applicable US law, which includes the ITSR [Iranian Transactions and Sanctions Regulations]' (US Department of Justice, 2019: 5). In other words, a Chinese national had been arrested on Canadian soil for violating US laws for engaging in business activities (outside of the US) with Iran, a state sanctioned by the US Department of Treasury. It could be argued that this case illustrates both the controversial nature of US extraterritorial sanctions (Terry, 2019), as well as the use of US offensive lawfare against the PRC (Goldenziel, 2020).

2.4.2 Lawfare through intergovernmental organisations

Intergovernmental organisations (IGOs) are fertile ground for the use of lawfare, or more specifically, multilateral lawfare. Their importance vis-à-vis lawfare is perhaps best illustrated with a metaphor: IGOs can be seen as a Swiss knife, that is as an instrument that contains multiple instruments. The rationale for it is unmysterious. IGOs provide a platform where states can utilise their legal instruments to achieve political aims of various types, such as obtaining territorial gains, weakening geopolitical rivals, altering the balance of power, or influencing the outcome of military conflicts – in most cases, without having to fire a single shot.

The very inception of the UN Security Council (UNSC) has been used as a paradigmatic illustration of the continuation of war by legal means. In Kennedy's view, this institution – the most powerful body of the UN system – was established by the victors of World War II[17] to institutionalise their newfound authority, empowering them to, *inter alia*, 'determine the legality of wars' (2012: 161). Additionally, the privileged position of the five permanent members of the UNSC allows them to enjoy an immense amount of institutional power, including crucial leverage over UN-based multilateral lawfare.

Indeed, the UNSC has the power to implement a wide range of measures, such as imposing arms embargoes, punishing states with multilateral financial sanctions (examined earlier), authorising military action, enforcing peace settlements, and establishing international criminal tribunals[18] to punish perpetrators of violence (Gowlland-Debbas, 2021). Kennedy uses the specific example of these special courts 'established by victors to adjudicate the criminality of opponents' as an argument to illustrate how law is, indeed, a continuation of war by non-violent means (2012: 160–161).

One of the most extreme lawfare instruments that can be imposed by the UNSC is that of 'No Fly Zones' (NFZs), which involve legally enforced military coercion. NFZs typically emerge in ongoing military contexts and are aimed at protecting civilian populations at risk by denying a given state the right to use its own airspace. Therefore, to a certain extent, they can be considered 'a de facto "occupation" of a state's sovereign airspace' (Schmitt, 2011: 47). One of the most important elements of NFZs is the enforcement, through legal means, of the prohibition of unauthorised aircraft, particularly military aircraft. It is important to note that the lawfulness of this instrument is subject to the support of a UNSC resolution (Schmitt, 2011; Zieliński, 2021). In recent decades, the UNSC has authorised imposing an NFZ in two conflicts: Bosnia and Herzegovina (1993) and Libya (2011). As seen previously, the latter case has been subjected to critiques and controversies of a legal nature. UNSC resolution 1973 authorised NATO to use 'all necessary measures', including an NFZ, to protect civilians (United Nations, 2011: 3). Critics, however, argue that NATO's implementation of the resolution was 'not consistent' with the UNSC mandate, as it prioritised conducting a regime change operation in Libya (illegal according to the UN Charter) over the protection of civilians (Kuperman, 2015: 113).

States can also pursue their interests using lawfare in a less militaristic and more diplomatic manner through another UN body, the International Court of Justice (ICJ). This UN organ has the authority to deal with two types of proceedings: contentious cases – disputes between states – and advisory opinions (International Court of Justice, 2022a). It has been argued that the ICJ is particularly prone to being strategically used (and abused) by states as a power-maximising instrument against their adversaries (Moore, 2012; Qureshi, 2019). In recent years, there has been an increase in territorial dispute proceedings aimed, in many cases, at expanding maritime rights through exclusive economic zones (Thirlway, 2018). Peru and Somalia, for example, have been able to legally widen their maritime boundaries as a result of the ICJ's rulings (International Court of Justice, 2014, 2021). These rulings have an impact not only in terms of sovereignty *in stricto sensu* but also in relation to control over resources, fishing rights, economic development, etc.

Perhaps one of the cases that best illustrates the power struggle through lawfare in the ICJ is the proceeding initiated by Nicaragua against the US in 1984. The ICJ ruling settled that the latter's support for paramilitary groups (commonly known as *the Contras*) as well as the laying of underwater mines in civilian ports in Nicaragua violated 'customary international law', specifically the prohibitions of 'not to use force against another State' and that of 'not to violate the sovereignty of another State' (International Court of Justice, 1986: 147). At first glance, this represented a resounding legal and geopolitical victory for Nicaragua. However, the US managed to mitigate this lawfare defeat by withdrawing from both this specific contentious case as well as from the ICJ's compulsory jurisdiction altogether (US Department of State, 1985). Washington put the final nail in the coffin[19] for this case in October 1986, when it vetoed a UNSC resolution which requested the US 'to comply with the ICJ ruling' (Keohane *et al.*, 2000: 474). Lawfare is, therefore, not immune from power hierarchies and, like with other instruments, great powers generally have the upper hand.

Lastly, we will succinctly examine the connection between lawfare and the International Criminal Court (ICC), an IGO outside the UN system established in 2002, primarily aimed at bringing to justice individuals involved in 'the gravest crimes of concern to the international community: genocide, war crimes, crimes against humanity and the crime of aggression' (2022). The ICC has been (as of 2022) ratified by 123 states.[20] Interestingly, there are notable exceptions among ratifiers, including three permanent members of the UNSC (the PRC, the US, and the Russian Federation) as well as powerful states such as India, Pakistan, and Turkey. Given that only individuals from a state party (or in a territory of a state party) can be prosecuted (International Criminal Court, 2022), a very likely explanation for such absences is the concern by these states that members of their militaries could be put on trial by the ICC.

This fear was accurately summarised by the US *National Defense Strategy* of 2005, which overtly asserted that the US would 'provide legal protections . . . against transfers of US personnel to the International Criminal Court' (US Department of Defense, 2005: 20). This can be seen as a defensive pre-emptive strategy to protect the US from lawfare conducted against it using ICC's legal instruments. In that regard, Goldsmith, one of the most notable critics of the ICC, deprecated the Court shortly after it came into force, by arguing that it was a legal tool instrumentalised by middle powers 'to limit the power of militarily superior nations' (2003: 101).

At any rate, the potential for lawfare actions within the ICC cannot be underestimated, because, as Tiemessen notes, 'ICC's judicial interventions are used as a tool of lawfare for States Parties . . . to pursue political ends' (2016: 414). In fact, the ICC served as an inspiration for Fisher and Stefan (2016) to develop the term 'International Criminal Lawfare'. One of the examples the aforementioned scholars used to build their argument was that of Ugandan President Yoweri Museveni, who in 2003 used the ICC to indict leaders from rebel groups:[21] that his army had failed to defeat through military means, to decimate and de-legitimise them (Fisher and Stefan, 2016). This brings us to our last lawfare method: rhetoric.

2.4.3 Discursive lawfare

Finally, we will shed light on discursive lawfare, that is, the rhetorical use of legal arguments to justify various foreign policies, including wars, military deployments, and targeted assassinations. This form of lawfare is closely connected to discursive power, defined by Ruggie as 'the ability to influence outcomes through promoting ideas, setting social norms and expectations' (2018: 325). While discursive lawfare is less visible and more subtle than other lawfare methods scrutinised in this chapter, it may have salient effects with regard to story-telling. In this section, we borrow from Ansah's (2010) work, which we deem the most comprehensive analysis of the intersection between lawfare and rhetoric. In Ansah's view, the law operates as a 'formal/instrumental expression' that provides legitimacy to 'different forms of violence' (2010: 92).

Legal justifications are, in effect, a central element when it comes to constructing successful foreign policy narratives, particularly in war contexts. This is hardly surprising as, more often than not, *legal* is directly associated with *legitimate* and, by the same token, *legality* often leads to *legitimacy*.[22] In the specific context of war, as Kennedy points out, 'perceptions about the law ... affect the legitimacy of the conflict as a whole' (2006: 156). While 'legal' and 'legitimate' are not technically synonyms, the conflation between both terms is etymologically rooted, as legitimacy directly translates as 'lawful' or 'in line with the law' in mediaeval Latin.

Suchman's famous definition conceptualises legitimacy as 'a generalized perception or assumption that the actions of an entity are desirable, proper, or appropriate within some socially constructed systems of norms, values, beliefs and definitions' (1995: 574). To put it simply, legitimacy is primarily connected with the morality of an action or, in our case, a policy. It is worth noting that legitimacy and morality are necessarily tied with the notion of hierarchy. This is well illustrated by the *Nicaragua v. the United States* case in the ICJ, seen earlier. As Carr bluntly puts it, international morality is 'a product of dominant nations' (1939/2016: 74). Similarly, Karagiannis argues that great powers have a tendency 'to reinterpret and redefine legal rules to serve national interests' (2014: 401). Building on Carr and Karagiannis's arguments, we contend that powerful states have more resources – financial, cultural, legal, and otherwise – to persuade other actors about the legitimacy of their actions. At any rate, legality and legitimacy are not synonyms nor equivalent, but this does not preclude the fact that they can work synergically and complementarily in the important enterprise of narrative building in international politics. As Max Weber eloquently put it a century ago: '[T]he most common form of legitimacy is the belief in legality' (1922/1968: 37).

This chapter has already highlighted some prominent examples of lawfare used as a discursive tool, for instance in the context of the importance of stating the lawfulness/unlawfulness of Chinese sovereignty claims in the SCS, or regarding the legal and normative critiques of Western military interventions by the Russian Federation. Additionally, in the Russian case, legal arguments played an important role in the context of attempting to justify Crimea's annexation in 2014. As Karagiannis notes, Moscow's emphasis on legal justifications served two main purposes: preventing potential legal challenges by Ukraine in international courts and protecting its international prestige (2014). The discursive use of lawfare is particularly pivotal when it comes to war contexts, for the simple reason that legal arguments are determinant to legitimise military operations through adherence/compliance, or the appearance of adherence/compliance, with the rule of law (Dunlap, 2008, 2009).

The importance of framing wars through legal arguments was, for example, particularly pervasive during the NATO intervention in Kosovo in 1999, to the extent that legal issues were 'one of the thorniest aspects of NATO's war against Yugoslavia' (Castan Pinos, 2019: 57). This is because, as critics have argued, NATO's *Operation Allied Force* was, indeed, illegal as it lacked UN Security Council authorisation (Said, 2000; Chomsky, 2008). To circumvent this illegality, the argument of – 'illegal but legitimate' – was used by supporters of the intervention (see e.g. Franck, 1999; Independent International Commission on Kosovo, 2000; Wheeler, 2000).

Barely a few years later after the intervention in Kosovo, the Bush administration went a step further and attempted to justify the Iraq war with the dubious legal argument that Baghdad had violated UN Security Council resolutions. However, as it has been cogently pointed out, no resolution authorised,[23] in any shape or form, the use of force against Iraq (Bellamy, 2004; Banta, 2008). More recently, the Trump administration spared no efforts to legally justify the assassination of Iranian General, Qasem Soleimani, conducted via a UAV strike in January 2020 in Baghdad. These legal justifications have been described as 'impossible to defend' (Haque, 2020) and as 'flawed' and 'dangerous' by an attorney-adviser from the US Department of State (Finucane, 2022). As Morrissey contends, Washington is no stranger to (discursive) lawfare as it has sought to 'legalise' the use of violence against those deemed as enemies in Iraq, Afghanistan and elsewhere (2011: 291).

Our final example illustrating the discursive use of lawfare to support political narratives in military contexts emanates from the often-neglected civil war in Yemen. In January 2022, Brigadier Yahya Sare'e, the spokesperson for the Yemeni armed forces,[24] announced that a vessel carrying United Arab Emirates' weapons aimed at a rival faction had been apprehended (2022). In addition to using arguments of a strategic military nature for seizing the cargo ship, Sare'e used a legal justification emphasising that the vessel had 'entered Yemeni waters without any license' (2022). This case, like the previous ones analysed in this chapter, illustrates how legal arguments are instrumental to legitimising military actions because, as argued by Ansah, the law operates – through lawfare – 'as a repository of value, reason' and 'truth' (2010: 101).

2.5 Conclusion

This chapter has shed light on the geopolitical dimension of lawfare, examining how great powers use a wide array of international legal instruments to pursue their national interests. Due to its importance, lawfare deserves to be considered a crucial foreign and defence policy tool that has the ability to consolidate and undermine established relations of power. Its flexibility allows states to apply it in conjunction with other tools and, in some cases, under the framework of IGOs. Further, lawfare is useful to develop narratives, and it is less financially costly and more discreet than other power instruments.

Further, the chapter has shown that geopolitical lawfare is being increasingly incorporated into the security strategy documents of the US, the PRC, and the Russian Federation, often as a method of hybrid warfare. This incorporation, however, significantly differs from country to country. The US is an interesting case because while it formally lacks a comprehensive lawfare strategy, it uses various lawfare methods profusely, so much so that one of these lawfare methods, sanctions, has become the most popular (coercive) foreign policy tool for Washington in recent years. Conversely, lawfare appears as a useful tool for the PRC and Russia for very specific aims, for instance to legitimise sovereignty and territorial claims as well as to challenge the US' global hegemony.

Lastly, while the geopolitical dimension is of paramount importance, it is not the only dimension of lawfare, nor the most controversial. The following chapter will recalibrate the focus to analyse a less scrutinised dimension: domestic lawfare, that is the use of lawfare by states in domestic contexts.

Notes

1 For his part, Foucault turned Clausewitz's statement around by stating that 'politics is war by other means' (2003: 15).
2 We examine conflicts involving non-state actors such as sub-national entities and civil society organisations in Chapters 4 and 5 respectively.

3 Sanctions, a lawfare instrument that will be discussed in this chapter, can of course generate a high degree of (less visible) mortality, as the Iraq example demonstrates. Various surveys indicate an increased level of the childhood mortality rate, caused by factors such as malnutrition and precariousness of the health system, following UNSC imposed sanctions in the 1990s (Ali and Shah, 2000).

4 The 2021 Biden administration's National Security Strategy is an interim document.

5 The absence of a formal US *strategy* for lawfare is somewhat paradoxical considering Dunlap's definition of the term as 'the strategy of using – or misusing – law' (2008: 146), provided at the beginning of this chapter.

6 For a complete and updated list of sanctioned entities and individuals worldwide, see US Department of Treasury, 2022a.

7 The armed forces of the PRC.

8 The SCS dispute involves the PRC and the US but also Vietnam, the Philippines, and other East Asian nations. Due to space constraints, the chapter will focus on the disputes between the two great powers.

9 It must be noted that the PRC did not participate in the arbitration and vowed not to accept the ruling nor to recognise it (Chinese Ministry of Foreign Affairs, 2016).

10 The Islands are claimed by various states, including the PRC, the Philippines, and Vietnam.

11 This refers to the instrument of international sanctions enacted, through extraterritorial jurisdiction, by the US.

12 Under Russian law, the territory is officially known as the 'Republic of Crimea and the Federal City of Sevastopol' since 2014 (Russian Ministry of Foreign Affairs, 2018). Conversely, the Ukrainian government typically describes the current status quo in Crimea as 'unlawful temporary occupation' (Ukrainian Ministry of Foreign Affairs, 2018).

13 As we will see in Chapter 4, the ICJ's *advisory opinion* concluded that 'international law contains no applicable prohibition of declarations of independence' (2010: 406).

14 The Wagner Group's official website (2022) surreptitiously acknowledges its participation in both war theatres.

15 The article provides specific details of punitive collective sanctions that shall be imposed against states resorting to wars of aggression: 'the severance of all trade or financial relations, the prohibition of all intercourse between their nationals and the nationals of the covenant-breaking State, and the prevention of all financial, commercial or personal intercourse between the nationals of the covenant-breaking State and the nationals of any other State' (League of Nations, 1919).

16 Nearly three years after her arrest, Meng eventually returned to China in 2021, following a diplomatic deal between Washington and Beijing (BBC, 2021a).

17 The US, the Soviet Union (since 1991, the Russian Federation), the Republic of China (since 1971, the PRC), France, and the UK. These five states are permanent members of the UNSC and enjoy veto power rights.

18 As of 2022, two have been established: the International Criminal Tribunal for the former Yugoslavia, or ICTY, (1993–2017) and the International Criminal Tribunal for Rwanda (1994–2016).

19 Despite the favourable ICJ ruling, Nicaragua did not receive any compensation, economic or otherwise.
20 That is states that have signed and ratified the Statute of Rome, the treaty that established the ICC.
21 It is understood that both the rebels from the Lord Resistance Army as well as Ugandan security forces had committed massacres and crimes against civilians (Branch, 2005). However, only members of the former were indicted by the ICC. Fisher and Stefan contend that this imbalance is explained by the fact that the ICC must rely on 'the goodwill of the government of the territory', and as a result, its decisions will necessarily be constrained and even compromised 'by politics' (2016: 246).
22 For a comprehensive scrutiny of the interplay between legality and legitimacy in the context of the nation-state, see Carl Schmitt's remarkable book *Legality and Legitimacy* (1932/2004).
23 The most compelling resolution was UNSC 1441 (United Nations, 2002). However, while the resolution condemned Iraq for breaching 'its obligations' and gave Saddam Hussein's government a 'final opportunity to comply with its disarmament obligations' (United Nations, 2002: 3), it did not authorise (not even implicitly) the use of force.
24 The Yemeni Armed Forces, one of the main belligerent parties in Yemen, is generally associated with the Ansarullah militia, commonly known as the Houthi movement. According to Saudi Arabia and the United States, the group has close ties with the Islamic Republic of Iran (Robinson, 2022).

Chapter 3

Domestic lawfare

3.1 Introduction

Domestic lawfare is arguably the most potentially pernicious variant of lawfare for liberal democratic systems. Our understanding of this dimension of lawfare draws on anthropologists Jean and John Comaroff, who defined lawfare as 'the resort to legal instruments, to the violence inherent in the law, to commit acts of political coercion' (2007: 144). Similarly, Gloppen's term 'state lawfare', which she conceives as the use of legal instruments by governmental actors to 'stay in power . . . by undermining the capacity of the opposition to contest elections' (2018: 7), is also highly valuable for our conceptualisation of domestic lawfare.

Thus, building on the Comaroffs (2001, 2006, 2007) and Gloppen (2018), we define domestic lawfare as *the strategy, pursued by domestic political actors, of using legal instruments to undermine their political opponents.* Our definition likewise shares some attributes with the conceptualisation of lawfare by Zanin *et al.*, who view this practice as 'the strategic use of the law with the purpose of delegitimizing, harming or annihilating the enemy' (2021: 7). This instrumentalisation of the law is typically carried out by governmental actors that aim to increase and accumulate political power and may include various tools such as (packed) courts, constitutional amendments, excessive litigation, or partisan legal interpretations.

To a certain extent, the famous dictum attributed to the late Brazilian President Getúlio Vargas epitomises the spirit of domestic lawfare: '[F]or my friends, everything; for my enemies, the law' (quoted in O'Donnell, 2004: 40). Domestic lawfare arguably undermines the independence of the judiciary as the courts have the potential of becoming subservient, and thus simply a useful vehicle for the

DOI: 10.4324/9781003289869-3

attainment of political aims by hegemonic actors. In turn, this can compromise the rule of law, one of the 'essential pillars upon which any high-quality democracy rests' (ibid.).

Although domestic lawfare is primarily used by governmental and state actors, it can also be used by parties in opposition as part of a strategy to bog down a government's legislative initiatives in the judicial mire. However, since domestic lawfare necessitates substantial resources and controlling the executive proves a stronger foundation to controlling the judiciary than being in opposition, it is more often employed by governmental or hegemonic actors, which is what we primarily focus on in this chapter.

In a similar caveat, we acknowledge that domestic lawfare is susceptible to emerge in any polity regardless of its nature. However, following our conceptualisation, domestic lawfare is a deeply embedded and structural practice used to perpetuate autocratic power in authoritarian regimes. As Moustafa and Ginsburg argue, the primary role of courts in authoritarian states is, *inter alia*, to 'establish social control and sideline political opponents' (2008: 8). The use of domestic lawfare instruments in authoritarian regimes is then in many respects ontological and endemic. This is the case because the very foundation of state institutions is aimed at perpetuating the power of those in power. The division of powers is, at best, a mere formality sometimes enshrined in the constitution albeit without any real impact. In other words, although any political system is arguably susceptible to domestic lawfare, in authoritarian regimes, it is a defining and intrinsic factor. Conversely, in liberal democracies, it is an exception that has the potential of hampering the liberal foundations of such regimes. In this chapter, we therefore focus on liberal democracies and the consequences for such polities when political actors engage in domestic lawfare.

Our understanding of domestic lawfare is highly indebted to Kirchheimer's concept of 'political justice'. The aim of political justice is to enlarge the area of political action by enlisting the services of courts on behalf of political goals (Kirchheimer, 2015: 419). What is and is not political is socially and culturally dependent, varying across time and different societies. Although Kirchheimer was surely interested in the motivation and strategy involved in 'political justice', his concept was much broader than what we here propose.[1] Instead, we aim for a narrower analytical concept of political repression through judicial means. We suggest domestic lawfare as an actor-centred term focusing on specific political strategies through legal instruments.

3.2 Related concepts

3.2.1 Judicialisation of politics

Domestic lawfare does not emerge abruptly nor *in vacuo*. Generally, it requires preconditions that pave the way for the practice to be successful. These preconditions, which concurrently operate as constituent elements, are a) the judicialisation of political conflicts and b) the loss of judicial independence. They may occur either simultaneously or in sequence. It is important to note that the existence of these preconditions in a given state does not inevitably lead to domestic lawfare. However, without them, it is very difficult to develop lawfare strategies, that is to use the law instrumentally to undermine political opposition. In addition to these two elements, domestic lawfare requires a more *active* element focusing on distinct political actors: law-based repressive strategies against opposition activists or policymakers. Therefore, domestic lawfare constitutes a valuable, actor-centred conceptual framework that complements judicialisation.

The judicialisation of politics is a concept that is connected to lawfare but, as Zanin *et al.* claim, they are not synonyms (2021). As pointed out earlier, it is not sufficient by itself to trigger domestic lawfare but constitutes an ideal condition for the emergence of lawfare. According to Ferejohn, this phenomenon has become quasi-global through practices involving the intervention of courts in policymaking processes such as limiting the authority of legislative institutions and, in turn, judicial organs exercising policymaking roles (2002: 41). Similarly, Hirschl argues that contemporary politics is experiencing a 'transition to juristocracy' (2011). Here, three major aspects of the judicialisation of politics can be identified:

> a) the spread of legal discourse, jargon, rules, and procedures into the political sphere
> b) the expansion of the judicial involvement in public policymaking
> c) the reliance on courts, judges, and the judicial system for dealing with politics.
>
> (Slaughter, 1999; Goldstein *et al.*, 2001; Hirschl, 2011)

The judicialisation of politics can be interpreted in two different ways. On the one hand, it can be viewed as the expansion of the role of the courts – or the judges – at the expense of the policymaker, that is, the transfer of decision-making rights from the legislature, the cabinet, or the civil service to the courts. This implies the spread of judicial decision-making methods outside the judicial province proper and an increasing reliance on courts to decide core moral predicaments, public policy questions, and political controversies (Hirschl, 2008: 2). On the other hand, if this judicialisation is accompanied by a loss of independence of the judiciary, it can lead to courts becoming instruments – not counterbalances – of the executive.

At any rate, judicialisation essentially involves turning politics into a form of judicial process. While judicialisation implies a process, domestic lawfare represents action. When this process is coupled with the loss of independence of the courts, the ground is fertile for domestic lawfare to emerge. Finally, domestic lawfare is also related to Landau's 'abusive constitutionalism' (2013) but differs in its analytical application. Where abusive constitutionalism focuses specifically on how would-be authoritarians use constitutional amendments and replacements leading to democratic erosion (ibid.:182), domestic lawfare is not limited to constitutional changes or indeed even to autocratic actors. Domestic lawfare can also be applicable to judicially induced democratic backsliding in states without a written constitution such as Israel (Sallon, 2005), Canada (Hunt, 2013), or the United Kingdom (Sunkin, 1994).

3.2.2 Power, law, and the state of exception

Domestic lawfare is essentially not a legal concept but a political instrument that speaks to a concerning trend in society. Our new conceptualisation of domestic lawfare is of course deeply indebted to other social theorists on law and politics, most notably the works of Michel Foucault and Giorgio Agamben.

Foucault never formulated a general theory of law and legal power (Hunt and Wickham, 1994; Brännström, 2014). He did, however, outline an approach to law and power that is useful for our development of the term domestic lawfare. As Foucault reminds us, political power not only resides with government institutions directly associated with the state but also exercises itself through the mediation of a number of institutions, 'which look as if they have nothing in common with the political power and as if they are independent of it, while they are not' (Chomsky and Foucault, 2015). Further, Foucault argues that the very idea of justice itself has been invented and put to work in different societies as an instrument of a particular political or economic power – or, as a weapon against such a power (ibid.).

According to Foucault, the birth of the modern liberal democratic state itself is tied to an understanding that juridical rationality would make it possible to define good and evil in all possible situations (2019b). Law was of course always political and political actors have always used law to further their aims. However, Foucault argues that *disciplinary* power has supplanted and even replaced judicial power as a primary mode of government (Hunt and Wickham, 1994). In Foucault's writings, law is receptive to the different forms of knowledge that infuse and inoculate it, as well as to the distinct historical assemblages of power that use the judiciary and deploy the law and legality to their own ends (2019a: 22). A general process in modern statecraft has led 'judges to judge something other than crimes; they have been led in their sentences to do something other than judge', with the law being integrated into contemporary processes of power (ibid.: 23).

Building on these insights, we advance the notion that domestic lawfare offers an instrumentalisation of Foucault's *legal governmentality*. The law is not passively being integrated into differently functioning power processes, nor is the increasing tendency that 'judges judge something other than crimes' (ibid) an unproblematic given. This bears strong resemblances to Marx and Engels arguments regarding law. In the *Communist Manifesto*, law in the bourgeois state is critically defined as a class instrument as Marx and Engels write '[Y]our jurisprudence is but the will of your class made into a law for all' (1955: 24).

Of course, power is intrinsically related to judicial mechanisms. Going by Foucault, power lays down the law; it prohibits, refuses, excludes, rejects, denies, obstructs, and occults. Domestic lawfare includes all these vital aspects of judicial politicking. Crucially, disciplinary power does not make the juridical institutions disappear or reduce legal acts. It rather encroaches upon and works through them (Brännström, 2014: 173). In other words, disciplinary power does not displace judicial power but co-opts it. In our conceptualisation, this process is (domestic) lawfare, which builds upon Foucault's understanding of norms, discipline, and judicial power. This furthers our understanding that the law is inherently subject to specific power assemblages, political aims, and interests. We do not mean to suggest that the judiciary is a neutral organism corrupted by political actors. Instead, we recognise that specific modes of domination are already inscribed in its design and mode of functioning. As such, acts of domestic lawfare can undermine the rule of law in a society and erode the legitimacy of the courts as arbiters.

Our conceptualisation of domestic lawfare also ties into Agamben's work on the state of exception (2005). The state of exception refers to political periods in which constitutional rights are diminished, super-seded, and rejected in the process of a government (or other powerful political actors) claiming such an extension of power. According to Agamben, modern totalitarianism can be defined as

> the establishment, by means of the state of exception, of a legal civil war that allows for the physical elimination not only of polit-ical adversaries but of entire categories of citizens who for some reason cannot be integrated into the political system.
>
> (ibid.: 2)

As explained earlier, we understand domestic lawfare as the process by which political actors use the judiciary to combat political opponents. This understanding is a useful concept that adds to Agamben's theories by unpacking the slippery slope process in which liberal democracies adopt authoritarian characteristics through the state of exception.

Similarly, although Agamben understands the state of exception as a political power superseding established laws and rights, we must also be attuned to how political actors can use courts, judges, and warrants to diminish and reject established political rules, and thereby turn what are essentially political struggles into legal issues. This is especially the case where the line between politics and the judiciary is thin, and where policymakers can exercise control and influence with judges and courts. Here, as Foucault argued, political power can be exercised through the mediating institution of the judicial system, while political opponents are bypassed, harassed, controlled, and eliminated through laws rather than democratic votes and public debates.

Domestic lawfare could be seen as political actors attempting to create a state of exception from *politics* in order to create apparently *apolitical* legal spaces in which they can further their political objectives without interference from political opponents. With Agamben and Foucault, we acknowledge that the state of exception can be achieved with the suspension of law. However, we argue that through domestic lawfare, such a state of exception can also be achieved by the judiciali-sation and the suspension of politics.

3.3 The effects of domestic lawfare on liberal democratic regimes

While domestic lawfare may have some beneficial effects in terms of power accumulation for actors who engage in it, it is not cost-free.

Politicised justice carries the germ of new dangers to liberal democracies, often exceeding the initial challenge in their severity (Kirchheimer, 2015: 172). One of its disturbing consequences is that courts run the risk of becoming a utopian institution, an arena in which to achieve political goals rather than justice, or what the Comaroffs have termed 'fetishism of law', which imposes order 'by means of violence rendered legible, legal, and legitimate by its own sovereign word' (2006: 30). In the face of political heterodoxy, legal instruments appear to offer politicians and civil servants a powerful repertoire of standardised terms and practices permitting values, beliefs, ideals, and interests to be negotiated across otherwise insurmountable political cleavages (ibid.).

However, the law is a social product, not an architect of social worlds and society. Therefore, powerful political actors can accomplish their goals through a judicialisation of the political, whereby they seek to render essentially political decisions objective and necessary. A law that violates basic democratic principles, such as removing elected officials from office, can be passed according to standard parliamentary procedures, conform to required forms and processes of transparency, and therefore be compliant with the rule of law. It is, nonetheless, seemingly inconsistent with the cornerstones of democratic polities.

Domestic lawfare represents political actors using the language of universal rights (and obligations) and ostensibly apolitical codes and laws to enact *political* verdicts. Domestic lawfare adequately highlights how political processes are held hostage by law and legal decisions, and how principally governmental actors deliberately use the judicialisation of politics to pursue political goals through judges, courts, and the legal system in general. For this to succeed, it is essential to pursue strategies aimed at reducing, compromising, and undermining the independence of the judiciary.

As Hamlin and Sala lucidly note, judicialisation is not inherently opposed to democratisation (2018: 4). Judicial checks and balances on elected officials, for example, expand democracy, and judicial empowerment is bound to take place wherever judicial review is adopted. The problem is that rather than protect the rule of law, domestic lawfare uses the mechanisms of constitutional change to erode the democratic order. In short, domestic lawfare represents a strategy that politicises law and judicialises politics. Through domestic lawfare, actors constrain opponents via control over the courts, the rewriting of laws, and the reinterpreting of codes and regulations for their own gain, all aided by appointing supporters to key legal institutions. Constitutional checks and balances are powerless to stop such abusive strategies, as the courts, legal codes, and judiciary are the very tools used by actors engaged in domestic lawfare.

The use of domestic lawfare in liberal democracies has multiple implications, not least the fact that it has the potential to undermine the very values and foundations such systems are built upon, potentially leading to what some authors have categorised as illiberal democracy (Zakaria, 2003), electoral authoritarianism (Bogaards, 2009), democratic backsliding (Bermeo, 2016) or de-democratisation (Kiely, 2017). A hybrid regime is a form of government that could be considered 'neither clearly democratic nor conventionally authoritarian' (Diamond, 2016: 151). The precise nature of the relationship between lawfare and these processes is highly complex and context-dependent. What is clear, however, is that the two are intrinsically connected.

This is illustrated by Bermeo's definition of democratic backsliding, which implies 'the state-led debilitation or elimination of any of the political institutions that sustain an existing democracy' (2016: 5). This emphasis on *institutional debilitation* shows the strong interconnection between domestic lawfare and democratic backsliding and draws our attention to the political actors that jeopardise democracy by weakening its institutional foundations. Domestic lawfare is therefore intertwined with democratic backsliding in liberal democracies as it can lead to the erosion of both democratic and legal institutions. Through the (ab)use and instrumentalisation of legal institutions, governmental actors engaging in domestic lawfare contribute to *institutional debilitation*, and consequently, to the erosion of existing checks and balances.

3.4 Applications of domestic lawfare

3.4.1 Soft domestic lawfare in Hungary and Poland?

The recent political-judicial developments in Hungary and Poland raise important and topical questions about the nature of democracy, legality, and political power. In our understanding, they represent softer or even pre-emptive versions of domestic lawfare, compared to more severe cases like those in Latin America, which we analyse next. This 'soft domestic lawfare' opens the door for the abuse and politicisation of the legal system and can have serious consequences for democratic backsliding and the independence of the judiciary.

Various authors have labelled Hungary a prime example of a 'hybrid regime', critically highlighting political actions from Hungary's executive that point in the direction of illiberalism (Bozóki and Hegedűs,

2018; Freedom House, 2022). Specifically, Cianetti *et al.* claim that since he got elected in 2010, Viktor Orbán's conservative-nationalist *Fidesz* party has sought to 'dismantle liberal checks and balances' in Hungary (2018: 244). The ruling party enacted a new electoral law in 2011 giving a competitive advantage to the party (Tóka, 2014: 324), and removed citizens' possibility to challenge the constitutionality of parliamentary laws in front of the Constitutional Court (Bogaards, 2018: 1486). As the former Hungarian President and leader of the Hungarian Constitutional Court, László Sólyom, has put it: '[T]he Constitution is used nowadays again merely as a tool of everyday politics' (2015). Such political reworkings of the rule of law are central to domestic lawfare.

Domestic lawfare is then distinguished from politicised litigation such as judicial activism or legal mobilisation, as it entails political actors attempting to hamstring political opponents through courts, litigation, constitutional amendments and replacements, or other politicised uses of law. Although elected political actors are expected to enact policies through legislation, domestic lawfare involves the strategic manipulation of legal instruments, including packing courts, selection of favourable judges, constitutional amendments, etc., to combat political opponents, leading to loss of judicial impartiality and erosion of elective democracy, or democratic backsliding.

This is arguably part of a global pattern of democratic regression through 'executive aggrandisement', where states are not breaking down into autocracy, but rather 'sliding' into some form of hybrid regime (Bozóki and Hegedűs, 2018), or illiberal democracy. In the Hungarian case, Fidesz rewrote hundred other pieces of legislation. While the majority of these changes addressed social and economic issues, Tóka argues that the philosophy that underlined them involved allowing the legislative majority and the executive to make decisive choices with as little constraint as possible (Tóka, 2014: 314). These electoral reforms avoided consensus building, followed the self-interest of the Fidesz party, and crucially, the partisan bias in the new law stems mainly from elements that cannot be called directly unconstitutional (ibid.: 325). Indeed, since Fidesz amended the Constitution as a private member's bill in 2012 in an act that Bogaards terms a 'constitutional coup d'état' (2018: 1481), the Constitutional Court appears to no longer be an effective check on the executive. Despite this, the *Fidesz* government has acted in a way that is at least procedurally consistent with the letter of the constitution (Bozóki and Hegedűs, 2018: 1177).

The measures taken by the Hungarian Fidesz party may not be strictly authoritarian, illegal, or unconstitutional, but they are examples of *doing* politics through judicial means, that is *soft* pre-emptive domestic lawfare. Symbolic hegemony, institutional domination, and selective, politicised readings of legal degrees are all pieces of the puzzle which Landau has termed 'abusive constitutionalism' (Landau, 2013: 212). Hungary's Constitutional Court has arguably lost its independence and no longer functions as a check on government, but as a tool of the same (Bogaards, 2018: 1488), leading to a deeply uneven political playing field where opponents of the Fidesz party are at a disadvantage (Bozóki and Hegedűs, 2018: 1177).

We term the developments implemented by the Hungarian executive as pre-emptive or *soft* domestic lawfare. By this, we mean that by gradually dismantling the rule of law, the ruling party has created the ideal conditions for future domestic lawfare actions aimed at undermining potential opposition. Unlike in Latin America, however, this form of *soft* lawfare has so far not led to harsher domestic lawfare actions such as the political arrests of opposition figures.

Several authors have pointed out that Poland is following a similar path to Hungary (Kelemen and Orenstein, 2016; Przybylski, 2018; Sadurski, 2018; Halmai, 2019). As we argue next, this necessarily has implications in terms of the dynamics of domestic lawfare. The leader of the Polish ruling party Law and Justice (PiS), Jarosław Kaczyński, illustrated the connection between Poland and the Hungarian model, asserting, 'The day will come when we will have Budapest in Warsaw[2]' (cited by The Economist, 2018).

While some authors have characterised the situation in Poland as 'unconstitutional populist backsliding' (Sadurski, 2018), others have gone further arguing that it can be considered an illiberal democracy engaged in practices reminiscent of 'illiberal constitutionalism' (Drinoczi and Bień-Kacała, 2019; Halmai, 2019). Halmai, for instance, claims that Poland – similar to Hungary – has, at least on paper, the institutions of a democratic constitutional state but that the power of these institutions has been undermined and their independence compromised (2019: 313). Such developments in soft domestic lawfare set the scene for harsher measures to emerge in Poland.

For instance, in a remarkable development, in July 2018, the Supreme Court was purged with the forced retirement of nearly 40% of its judges, including the president of the Court (Santora, 2018). Sadurski denounces that the dismantlement of constitutional checks and balances was carried out in two stages: first the Constitutional Tribunal was rendered powerless through paralysation by PiS in late 2015 and, subsequently, once the ruling party gained control over it, the tribunal was positively used 'against the opposition' (2018: 17–18). The instrumental use of courts to undermine political rivals and empower the ruling party is a crucial element of domestic lawfare, and such developments establish the necessary conditions for the judicial undermining of political opponents.

Amnesty International has pointed out that as a result of the judicial reforms that subject 'the judicial branch to political pressure from the executive branch, it is unclear whether Poland's judiciary will be in a position to continue to uphold and guarantee the right to peaceful assembly' (2018: 24). The legal procedures against anti-government demonstrators (see Amnesty International, 2018; Drinoczi and Bień-Kacała, 2019) may be seen as incipient yet important examples of domestic lawfare being used to protect and perpetuate the power of the ruling party at the expense of not only political opponents, but also fundamental citizens' rights.

Last but not least, it is worth noting that Poland has faced EU proceedings for the seemingly illiberal reforms it has implemented over the past few years. In December 2017, the EU Commission sent a proposal to the Council stating that there was a 'clear risk of a serious breach by the Republic of Poland of the rule of law' (European Commission, 2017: 1), primarily related to its lack of judicial independence, and activated Article 7(1) TEU. Interestingly, disputes between the European Commission and a member state through this judicial mechanism, which can result in sanctions and temporary deprivation of voting rights for the affected state, bear strong resemblances to the geopolitical dimension of lawfare explained in the previous chapter.

The argument of lack of judicial independence was used, in March 2020, as an argument by a regional German court to refuse the extradition of a suspect from Germany to Poland (Bauomy, 2020). Similar to the Hungarian case, developments in the form of power concentration in the hands of the executive in Poland constitute a *soft* form of domestic lawfare, clearing the way for the potential implementation of this practice in the future.

3.4.2 Domestic lawfare in Latin America

Latin America is perhaps the area in the world where the term lawfare has permeated political debates most thoroughly. This is illustrated by the notoriously high number of Google searches for the term from

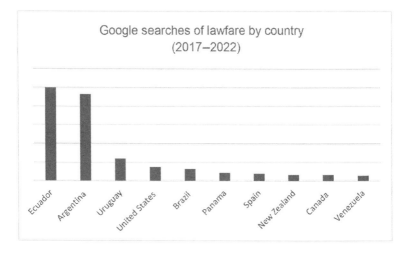

Figure 3.1 Google searches of lawfare by country

Source: elaborated by authors based on Google Trends data

that region (see Figure 3.1). The prominence of discussions over this practice has led to the establishment of academic institutions, such as the Lawfare Institute (based in Brazil) and the Lawfare Observatory CELAG (based in Argentina), exclusively focused on the scrutiny of different facets of lawfare in Latin America. Additionally, in December 2021, the Argentinian government organised a conference with hundreds of scholars, policymakers, and activists to discuss the impact of domestic lawfare on human rights (Gobierno Argentino, 2021).

However, the existence of domestic lawfare in Latin America is not universally accepted. On the one hand, some view it as a 'conspiracy theory' (Clarín, 2021), or as an attempt to victimise and exonerate 'populist' policymakers involved in 'corruption' cases (Hidalgo Andrade, 2018). On the other hand, a significant number of scholars and pundits contend that this practice has played a pivotal role in the region, resulting in the incarceration and exile of leading political figures and the alteration of electoral processes (Vollenweider and Romano, 2017; Romano, 2020; Tirado, 2021; Zanin *et al.*, 2021). Lawfare is, in that sense, both a contested term and simultaneously an element that deepens the political polarisation between progressive and conservative actors in Latin America.

Brazil and Ecuador are generally highlighted as examples of countries where domestic lawfare has been triggered (Calderón Castillo, 2018; Tirado, 2021). The former is particularly relevant. In 2017, former President Luiz Inácio Lula da Silva (2003–2010) was sentenced to nearly ten years in prison, following a controversial trial at a lower court which found him guilty of money laundering and corruption for allegedly taking bribes from the state oil company, 'Petrobras' (BBC, 2017a). His legal team argued, from the onset of the process, that this prosecution constituted a clear case of lawfare aimed at the destruction of a political enemy (Zanin[3] et al., 2021). Likewise, Lula's supporters – including former President Dilma Roussef (2011–2016) – used the term lawfare in social media to denounce the politically motivated character of Lula's conviction (Rousseff, 2020). In the same vein, numerous scholars have applied the notion of lawfare to the Lula case, emphasising that prosecutors (and the judge) used law as a weapon, that is, as an instrument of political repression (Ribeiro, 2018; Romano, 2020; Guardiola-Rivera, 2021).

Lula's sentence had immediate political consequences, namely he was unable[4] to contest the 2018 presidential elections where he was the frontrunner against Jair Bolsonaro, who ended up winning the race. Adding to the controversy, Bolsonaro appointed the lower court judge who convicted Lula, Sérgio Moro, as Justice Minister as soon as he took office (Phillips, 2018). According to an investigative report from *The Intercept*, leaked documents reveal that Moro and the lead prosecutor deliberately colluded to find the most effective way to 'structure the corruption case against Lula', with the explicit aim of preventing a presidential victory (Greenwald and Pougy, 2019). The argument that Lula's conviction primarily responded to a domestic lawfare logic gained significant momentum in 2021, when Brazil's Supreme Court annulled his corruption convictions on the grounds that the court that tried him lacked jurisdiction (BBC, 2021b).

Similar to Brazil, in Ecuador the alleged use of domestic lawfare has directly involved top political figures, such as former President Rafael Correa (2007–2017). In a plot that resembles a Hollywood thriller, in July 2018, a judge from Ecuador's high court ordered Correa's arrest for allegedly masterminding the kidnapping of an opposition lawmaker in 2012 (BBC, 2018). In addition, Correa faces at least ten additional counts, mainly connected to corruption (Romano, 2020).

Critics argue that Correa's prosecution, like Lula's, was primarily aimed at preventing his return to politics, through the use of a kangaroo court that used 'false witnesses' and 'lacked evidence' (Calderón

Castillo, 2018). Striffler has denounced that Correa's successor, former President Lenin Moreno (2017–2021), developed a lawfare strategy which involved 'perverting the legal system in order to subvert the democratic process' (2020). Correa himself has argued that the objective of lawfare in Ecuador is to 'neutralise' progressive leaders 'through juridical means to accomplish through courts what they could not accomplish through the ballot box' (2021). Since 2018, Interpol has refused to arrest Correa (who lives in exile in Belgium) three times alleging that the case is 'obviously a political matter' (Deutsche Welle, 2018; Europa Press, 2021).

Finally, several authors argue that the use of domestic lawfare practices in Latin America cannot be understood in isolation but rather forms part of a 'regional strategy' (Romano, 2020; Correa, 2021; Tirado, 2021), aimed at influencing not only political dynamics in specific governments but at shifting the geopolitical balance of power of the region. This hints at the interconnectedness of the different dimensions of lawfare that we outline in this book, namely geopolitical and domestic lawfare, as well as the sub-dimension state lawfare that we analyse in the following chapter.

3.5 Conclusion

To sum up, domestic lawfare represents a strategy that politicises law and judicialises politics, potentially leading to severe democratic erosion. This does not necessarily imply that hegemonic political actors outright break the law, but rather that they infiltrate it, expand its purview, and bend the heavily politicised legal system to their will to mobilise it against their political adversaries. Through domestic lawfare, hegemonic actors constrain opponents via control over the courts, the rewriting of laws, and the reinterpreting of codes and regulations for their own gain, all aided by appointing supporters to key legal institutions.

This dimension of lawfare has the potential to severely weaken the rule of law and threaten the independence of the judiciary, which are inherent and crucial aspects of democratic erosion. Further, as domestic lawfare can undermine the capacity of the opposition to contest elections (Gloppen, 2018: 7), it also has serious implications for undermining the 'free' and 'fair' nature of electoral processes in democratic regimes. Unlike in authoritarian regimes, where this practice is endemic, domestic lawfare is rare in liberal democracies and undermines essential elements of these regimes.

As evidenced by our short case studies in Europe and Latin America, the precise nature of the relationship between domestic lawfare and processes of illiberalisation or democratic backsliding is highly complex and context-dependent. Further, both soft and harsher versions of domestic lawfare exist, varying significantly in severity and coerciveness. While the 'soft' domestic lawfare developments in Hungary and Poland pave the way for more severe measures, the domestic lawfare in the Latin American cases have resulted in actual political incarcerations such as that of former Brazilian President Lula and the exile of former Ecuadorian President Rafael Correa. This explains why, as we claimed at the beginning of this chapter, domestic lawfare is the most potentially pernicious dimension of lawfare.

Another important aspect of domestic lawfare is state lawfare, a subvariant primarily used by central state actors with the specific aim of safeguarding the territorial integrity of the state against secessionist or national minorities. This is where we turn to next, in Chapter 4.

Notes

1 Kirchheimer's political justice covered such diverse topics as colonial powers ruling through legal systems that exclude local majorities, the illegalisation of the Communist Party in the US in the 1950s, and the politicised elasticity of the judge appointments in the German Democratic Republic (2015).

2 Russia's invasion of Ukraine in February 2022 may have sabotaged the harmonious relationship between both central European governments. This is explained by their diametrically opposed views regarding policy responses to Moscow (see Przybylski, 2022).

3 Cristiano Zanin and Valeska Martins, two of the authors of *Lawfare: Waging war through law* (Routledge, 2021), coordinated the legal defence of former President Lula.

4 The UN Human Rights Committee unsuccessfully requested the Brazilian government to allow Lula to contest the 2018 presidential elections (Human Rights Council, 2018).

Chapter 4

Lawfare and territorial conflicts

4.1 Introduction

As we discussed in the previous chapter, domestic lawfare may carry significant risks to any liberal democratic system since the application of that type of lawfare tends to go from the particular to endemic. In this chapter, we focus on a sub-dimension of domestic lawfare with its own particularities and consequences for democratic politics: state lawfare in internal territorial conflicts. This is one of the areas in which governments are most likely to employ state lawfare, given the power asymmetry in favour of the central state.

Such conflicts often take place against a backdrop of divided loyalties and competing politico-legal systems where two polities lay claim to the same territory, as in the case of secessionist movements. States of exception, special orders, incarceration of political and civil society leaders, and temporary loss of civil liberties are all key elements of how governments employ state lawfare to 'solve' disputes with minority territorial groups. While these measures may be effective, they also have the potential to aggravate the conflict in the long run by creating additional grievances that complicate the resolution of the territorial dispute.

Due to the scarcity of literature focusing on state lawfare applied to territorial disputes, this chapter is particularly relevant and contributes critically to the conceptualisation of lawfare. To shed light on this dimension of state lawfare, in this chapter we discuss the concept of rule of law and survey key territorial conflicts in which governments used state lawfare. Practices of state lawfare in liberal democracies reveal important contradictions and incongruencies that could challenge the very nature of the political system. Consequently, in this chapter we focus exclusively on these regimes. Specifically, our

DOI: 10.4324/9781003289869-4

empirical cases include the US legal dispossession of Native Americans and the more recent cases of the United Kingdom using state lawfare in the ethno-nationalist conflict in Northern Ireland and Spain against the secessionist movements in the Basque Country and Catalonia.

These case studies, while not meant to be exhaustive, illustrate the blurring of civil and security or military elements produced by state lawfare. Rather, when governments use lawfare to quell secessionist groups in territorial conflicts, the tendency is for them to frame violence as legal measures on one hand, and on the other to justify arbitrary judicial practices with the language of war. Such a strategy has the consequence of legalising violence and martialising the law, complicating political compromise since one's political opponents have been turned into enemy combatants. This intersection of the civil and the security approach is characteristic of state lawfare and represents part of the reason why this term is a powerfully intuitive heuristic.

Before moving on to the case studies, we first discuss how the judicial concept of rule of law can further an understanding of the dynamics of state lawfare in internal territorial conflicts.

4.2 Rule of law in territorial conflicts

A crucial element of state lawfare is the concept of rule of law, understood as compliance with the institutional rules that define a political system. This is particularly salient in internal territorial conflicts, which is why we discuss it before presenting the case studies in this chapter. Rule of law, if identified with a point of ideal justice where all citizens are treated equally, is – strictly speaking – unattainable. As Holmes points out, although no legal system treats all citizens equally, rule of law can be approximated by 'expanding the circle of those able to protect their interests reliably by legal means' (2003: 22). This line of reasoning is inspired by Rousseau, who argued that liberal justice and the rule of law can be approximated by roughly equal groups making up a large proportion of the population, with all of them gaining some political leverage (ibid.). A pluralistic society, then, is the closest we come to the rule of law. On the other hand, *asymmetrical pluralism*, where politically influential groups receive better legal protection than members of politically insignificant groups, is detrimental to the rule of law.

For this reason, state lawfare is likely to emerge in internal territorial conflict where there is a fundamental degree of power asymmetry between the territorial minority and the central state. This hegemony of the central state is most visible in the legal domain, since regardless of the (local) political capital and force (popular support, electoral seats, etc.), the law will always be on the majority government's side. Further, as Sánchez-Cuenca reminds us, laws cannot rule by themselves but are subject to human agency (2003: 62). Simply put, the 'rule of law' merely means that rulers are bound by the law and must comply with it.

The law, being a social, political, and cultural construct, is the subject of human agency and can always be ignored, discarded, violated, or suspended based on political circumstances (ibid.: 63). Such a contingent understanding of legality is important to avoid legalism. This means that any rule of law does not imply that the law rules over people. Rather, rule of law is when the political actors in a given system have no interest in subverting the current institutional order and political system (ibid.: 63). This is a key reason why lawfare is salient in territorial conflicts, as by definition, secessionist movements seek to subvert the given territorial-institutional order and establish another in its place in the form of a new state.

Audre Lorde memorably stated that the master's tools will not dismantle the master's house (2018). This is likewise the case with secession movements. Here Searle's distinction between regulative and constitutive rules can further an understanding of state lawfare in internal territorial conflicts (2018). *Regulative* rules regulate pre-existing forms of behaviour while *constitutive* rules make possible new forms of behaviour and constitute the very phenomena they regulate (ibid.: 51). There are very few states whose legal framework includes the right of self-determination for minorities or the possibility to secede. The constitutions which, at least formally, enshrine that right – Ethiopia, St Kitts and Nevins, Uzbekistan and Lichtenstein – are anomalous (Constitution of the Republic of Uzbekistan, 2003; Radan, 2012; Bossacoma, 2020). As we elaborate later, following the 1998 Good Friday Agreement, Northern Ireland also constitutes an exception, as said treaty recognises the right of self-determination for Northern Irish citizens (Castan Pinos & Sacramento, 2020).[1]

Despite these exceptions, territorial-secessionist conflicts generally exist in the realm of politico-judicial struggle as they are essentially political struggles pushed into the legal domain. The central state may enact regulative laws that hinder for example the proclamation of a new statehood for a given territory, as is the case in most constitutions, but conversely no legal mechanisms exist for a territorially based secessionist movement to legally complete their political objective. Some institutional accommodation is, of course, possible; political rewards such as power, information, influence, or honour allows the system to produce some institutional selective incentives that reinforce the existing rules of the game (Sánchez-Cuenca, 2003: 86). This means the system can placate dissidents by incorporating them into the existing power structures. In the case of territorial conflicts, this process is possible yet inherently complicated.

However, in the face of irredentist demands that go beyond autonomy, such as secession, the whole political ontology of the unitary state is questioned. Here, an institutional accommodation is virtually impossible, perhaps barring the establishment of a deeply decentralised federal system, which fundamentally changes the nature of the polity and the power structures that condition it. Such fundamental changes – even in the few cases in which there is political will to enact them – are however made difficult due to the institutional inertia of constitutive rules. As Tsebelis has outlined regarding policy stability, the greater number of veto players required to change rules, the greater the institutional stability of the rules (1995).

Constitutive rules, such as a constitution, have more institutional inertia than ordinary laws because the number of veto players involved in constitutional reform is higher due to qualified majorities, the concurrence of several branches of power, popular referenda, etc. (Sánchez-Cuenca, 2003: 89). A constitution is of course designed to be stable and difficult to change, but when the constitution is not built upon a solid foundation of political compromise, this inertia becomes a hindrance for successful accommodation of political difference and can lead to state lawfare. This is especially the case in territorial conflicts where competing constitutive rules are at play and where the hegemonic judicial and executive interests of the central state will tend to align as the very territorial integrity of the state is at stake. According to Dworkin, when judges are called upon to decide fundamental legal-political conflicts, they attempt to take positions that best reflect a given country's political and intellectual moral traditions and are therefore disposed to follow the government (1970: 153).

The very state apparatus involved in a territorial conflict will then have the legal authority to decide controversial legal and constitutional issues. This is perhaps a necessity, but we must recognise that such a rule of law does *not* imply impartial fairness as it is subject to politics. On some occasions, state lawfare applied to territorial conflicts can also occur in international courts. When this happens, the state no longer enjoys a legal monopoly and, as a result, the level of uncertainty exponentially increases. This is illustrated by the Kosovo case, in which Serbia requested an advisory opinion from the International Court of Justice to determine the legality of Kosovo's unilateral independence (United Nations, 2008). The objective of this lawfare strategy was to legally undermine Kosovo's independence through a non-binding – yet politically significant – opinion from an UN court. The strategy, however, ended up being totally counterproductive (Castan Pinos, 2015, 2019), given that the court concluded that Kosovo's independence 'did not violate . . . international law' (International Court of Justice, 2010: 53).

We now move on to concrete empirical examples of state lawfare in territorial conflicts, showing the intertwining of martial, political, and legal elements in these conflicts. Additionally, our cases illustrate the negative consequences for democratic stability and liberal rights when hegemonic actors seek to move inherently political conflicts to the legal domain.

4.3 The legal dispossession of Native Americans

4.3.1 Situation

One of the most notorious cases of state lawfare used in territorial conflicts is the territorial dispossession of Native Americans during the 19th century US westward expansion. In many ways, this can be considered the paradigmatic case of use of state lawfare in territorial conflicts. It is therefore hardly surprising why Comaroff originally used this case to conceptualise lawfare as 'the effort to conquer and control indigenous peoples by the coercive use of legal means' (2001: 306).

To situate this territorial dispossession and what has been categorised as a US 'assault on indigenous sovereignty' (Saunt, 2020: xiv), we will succinctly summarise the most salient lawfare instruments employed by US courts to legally enact territorial usurpations. Few cases show the callous effectiveness of legal instruments in internal territorial conflicts as the so-called Marshall Trilogy of court cases. The Marshall Trilogy was composed of three US Supreme Court Rulings. The first, *Johnson v. McIntosh*, 1823, held that private citizens could not purchase lands from Native Americans (US Supreme Court, 1823). The second, *Cherokee Nation v. Georgia*, 1831 stipulated that the Cherokee nation was dependent on the United States as a 'ward to its guardian' (US Supreme Court, 1831). Lastly, *Worcester v. Georgia*, 1832, stated that the federal government was the sole authority in dealing with Indian nations (US Supreme Court, 1832). Together, these laws established the foundations of American Federal Indian Law (Pappas, 2017: 24) and cemented the relationship between Native American nations and the US state.

4.3.2 Analysis

In perhaps the most prominent case, the case of *Johnson v. McIntosh*, 1823, the United States Supreme Court affirmed that Native Americans could occupy and control US lands but could not hold title to them, and therefore had no legal claims to territory (US Supreme Court, 1823). Crucially, where earlier dealings and treaties with native peoples treated these as foreign nations, any zone of 'Indian jurisdiction' was now a violation of US state sovereignty under Article IV, Section 3 of the constitution.[2]

Native Americans could either be seen as sovereign states, which violated the US constitution, or as subjects of US law and territorial jurisdiction. In both cases, they had no claim to the territory they lived on, and the US government could dispose of these lands as they saw fit, as no distinction was made between vacant land and land occupied by Indians (Pappas, 2017: 53). This included the wholesale removal of entire Indian nations from the east to the central United States and the confiscation and exploitation of remaining Indian lands and resources leading to Native American communities becoming isolated on reservations or chequered parcels of detached lands in destitute regions (Fletcher, 2014).

Through the Indian Appropriations Act of 1871 and the subsequent affirmation of this Act by the Supreme Court in *United States v. Kagama, 1886* (US Supreme Court, 1886), Congress was granted plenary power over all Native American tribes within US borders and allowed the federal government to interact with tribes through acts of Congress rather than treaties. This effectively removed Native American nations as distinct political actors with whom the government had to bargain and negotiate and turned Native Americans into subjects of the state without particular territorial claims and without political representation. This alliance between the judiciary and the political arm of the US government allowed for the widespread claiming of tribal land. Their territorial dispossession was indeed enforced through legal coercion, which in turn created a legal trap: the US constitution allowed federal governments to repress any 'insurrection' if native peoples resisted state authority (Saunt, 2020: 40). As argued earlier, this case epitomises the use of territorial lawfare and its salient implications for sovereignty and political compromise.

4.3.3 Implications

Power has been typically understood as a zero-sum game by international relations scholars (Christensen, 2006; Mearsheimer, 2021). In this particular case, this logic appears quite obvious illustrating how one side was disempowered, expelled from its ancestral lands, and territorially dispossessed in benefit of the other.

It seems evident that in the cases analysed previously, the US Supreme Court transcended its role as a judicial tribunal and found itself 'ruling as aspiring philosopher kings' (Goetting, 2008: 1), placing the most basic rights of minority groups in jeopardy. The territorial dispossession of Native Americans through legal means perfectly illustrates that the use of state lawfare to pursue territorial objectives can be brutally effective as a blunt instrument of hegemonic disciplinary power, irrespective of moral considerations. This legal-based usurpation of sovereignty had implications that went well beyond the US. In the view of Saunt, this case became an inspiration and 'a model for colonial empires around the world' (2020: xv).

4.4 State lawfare in Northern Ireland

The Native American case analysed earlier is extraordinary but by no means exceptional. State lawfare is also used by other states challenged by territorial contestation. The next section will shed light on the state lawfare instruments employed by the UK government in Northern Ireland during the so-called Troubles. This case is interesting for various reasons, not least due to the fact that the state repression based on lawfare was conducted by a stable liberal democracy, typically considered as a free polity that guarantees civil freedoms and liberties (White and Falkenberg White, 1995).

4.4.1 Situation

The violent modern territorial conflict in Northern Ireland, popularly known as 'the Troubles', lasted from the late 1960s to 1998, when a peace process culminated with the signing of the Good Friday Agreement. Described as an 'irregular' (Schaeffer, 1999: 152) or low-level war (Hennessey, 1999: 42), the Troubles have been interpreted as an ethnonational conflict (McGarry, 1995) with territoriality at its core: 'republicans have aimed at achieving a united Ireland by excluding British rule from Northern Ireland, while the loyalists' objective has been to prevent Northern Ireland from being forced into a united Ireland' (Drake, 1998: 63). Poetically put, the six northern counties of Ireland were simultaneously the prize over which the parties fought, and the arena of the conflict.

The Irish Republican contestation of the British government-enacted partition of Ireland into two states in 1921, which led to the creation of a new political entity, Northern Ireland, is arguably one of the central causes of the conflict (Castan Pinos and McCall, 2021). While it was not the first time that Irish Republican militants, such as the Irish Republican Army (IRA), initiated an armed campaign against the partition of the island, with over 3,500 deaths, the Troubles in Northern Ireland was 'the most lethal . . . with at least twice as many casualties as in the Irish War of Independence' (ibid.: 852).

The complex conflictual dynamics involving numerous illegal and semi-legal paramilitary groups and considerable levels of political violence presented a daunting challenge for the British security forces. On some occasions, the British state apparatus resorted to state lawfare strategies that generated legally grey zones in a conflict that already housed clashes of jurisdiction. Chief amongst them was the so-called *Operation Demetrius* by the British Army and the policy of 'internment', that is the wide scale detentions without trials that followed it.

After consulting with Prime Minister Edward Heath, Unionist leader Brian Faulkner introduced internment on 9 August 1971, to combat what was seen as the rising threat of Irish Republican terrorism and, in turn, to deal with a threat to the territorial status quo. The decision to introduce these extrajudicial measures were taken at the highest level of the UK government, and British government ministers were possibly even informed about the use of torture in the interrogations of suspected IRA members (Hennessy, 2021). For nearly 15 months (from August 1971 to November 1972), the so-called Special Powers Regulations were in effect, granting authorities in Northern Ireland four extrajudicial powers:

(i) *arrest for interrogation purposes during 48 hours*
  (ii) *arrest and remand in custody*
  (iii) *detention of an arrested person*
  (iv) *internment*

(ECHR, 1978)

On the same day as the Special Powers Regulations were put into effect, 3,000 troops were sent out in 'Operation Demetrius' to strike a blow to the Republican insurgents, which resulted in 342 arrests (O'Boyle, 1977: 675). These arrests were controversial and legally problematic for numerous reasons, not least because many of the detainees had little or no connection to the IRA or other violent Republican groups. British Army Colonel Michael Dewar later admitted that the net of detainees had been cast far too wide, with internees ranging 'from known terrorists to comparatively harmless pamphleteers' (1996: 53).

This legal exceptionality effectively meant that in addition to the ordinary criminal law which remained in force in Northern Ireland, the authorities had various other discretionary powers at their disposal, enabling them to 'effect extrajudicial deprivation of liberty', or indefinite internment without trial (ECHR, 1978). Challenging internments legally was close to impossible; no legislation conferred the right to prisoners of having their detention reviewed. Safeguards were nominal, falling short of what the European Convention Article 5 deems 'lawful detentions' (Dickson, 2009: 932). Additionally, detainees could not complain to the European Commission of Human Rights about such breaches of Article 5 of the European Convention because the UK had been delaying the ratification of this Article since 1957 with the pretext of a 'public emergency' – and continued to delay ratification in Northern Ireland until finally ratifying the Article in 2000 (ibid.).

Although the government of Northern Ireland was suspended in February 1972, the British government continued with the internment policy until 5 December 1975, renaming them as 'detentions'. Between August 1971 and December 1975, a total of 1,981 people were interned, in quite disproportionate numbers: 107 Loyalists and 1,874 Irish Republicans. The number of internees reached its peak in late March 1972, coinciding with the peak of political violence in Northern Ireland, when 924 people were held at the same time (Rosland, 2009: 316).

The extrajudicial coercive strategy, based on state lawfare, practised in Northern Ireland had serious consequences for the conflict. The British authorities defended the introduction of internment as a necessary means to control the escalating conflict in Northern Ireland and curtail the violence. Hayes *et al.* highlight that while internment was a 'desperate attempt to bring order to a society increasingly undermined by conflict', it paradoxically had the opposite effect (2005: 15). In the two years prior to internment, 66 people were killed in the conflict, while this number rose almost tenfold to 610 in only the first 17 months of internment (Dixon, 2008: 118). Importantly, the fateful Bloody Sunday massacre, where 14 unarmed civilians were killed by British paratroopers in Derry (see House of Commons, 2010), was precisely an anti-internment march, which would have far-reaching consequences for the conflict. By the end of 1975, more than 1,300 people had died in the now escalated violence (Rosland, 2009: 316).

The policy of internment, which was immensely unpopular with the Irish Catholic population, led to a sharp increase in violence and displaced 7,000 people from their homes in some of the worst Protestant-Catholic riots of the 20th century (Coogan, 2002: 152). A long-term by-effect of the British state lawfare was the damage done to the relationship between the Catholic Irish community and the RUC and British Army. Internments ensured continuous enlistment in the hardline Provisional IRA (PIRA) (Dickson, 2009: 938), which built itself into a strong and well-organised military force (Boyle et al., 1975: 56; Coogan, 2002: 153). The PIRA and other Republican groups benefited from increased hostility to British troops in Catholic communities, pushing even moderates into a profound rejection of the authority of the British state (Hamill, 1985: 65; O'Dochartaigh, 2005: 235). As a result of the state lawfare, recruitment and financial support for Republican paramilitaries rose dramatically and large-scale guerrilla warfare became a mainstay of the conflict (Farrell, 1976; Smith, 1997; O'Doherty, 1997).

In hindsight, internment emerged as a profoundly ineffective way of dealing with the conflict in Northern Ireland, promoting generalised resentment in the population and arguably escalating violence. It is also questionable from a moral and a legal-philosophical standpoint. We see it as a paradigmatic case of state lawfare in territorial conflicts due to the authorities' intentional and deliberate blurring of judicial and military boundaries to gain leverage over a perceived opponent in spite of the human and democratic costs.

4.4.2 Analysis

The legally grey zones of the conflict in Northern Ireland spilled over into diplomatic controversy when the government of Ireland filed an interstate application against the United Kingdom with the European Commission of Human Rights[3] in 1971 (Cohn, 1979: 159). Following the case, the UK admitted to using the so-called five techniques of prolonged wall-standing and stress-positions, continuous hooding of detainees when not being interrogated, subjection to loud noise, sleep deprivation, and deprivation of food and drink (Greenwood, 1980: 198). These techniques were applied with the intent to cause intense physical and mental suffering. While the European Court of Human Rights (ECHR) conceded that there had existed an 'administrative practice of inhuman treatment' and concluded that the 'five techniques' constituted a breach of the European Convention on Human Rights, it ruled that this practice did not match the necessary intensity and cruelty of the word 'torture' (ECHR, 1978).

Internment and the wider policy of state lawfare is done by authorities when the ordinary processes of law and order are deemed too slow or cumbersome. Legal protections or the rule of law are therefore seen as *impediments* to handling the conflict, which can be dispensed with in the name of security. As Dickson points out, the grounds for internment have historically often been easily satisfied, with little opposition in British Parliaments or cabinets (2009: 931). The blurring of the civil and the martial in governmental applications of state lawfare are evident in the contemporary framing of the conflict. In the public statement on August 10, wherein he introduced the policy of internment and 'Operation Demetrius', Brian Faulkner, leader of the Ulster Unionist Party and Prime Minister of Northern Ireland, all but explicitly stated the use of state lawfare:

> We are, quite simply, at war with the terrorists and in a state of war many sacrifices have to be made. . . . I have had to conclude that the ordinary law cannot deal comprehensively or quickly enough with such ruthless violence.
>
> (BBC, 1971)

This framing of the violent domestic conflict as war, coupled with the explicit statement that it lies outside the reach of 'ordinary law', marks this as a clear example of a state of exception (cf. Agamben, 2005), in which those in power come to decide the law. Despite this, internments and other far-reaching extrajudicial curtailments of civil liberties were consistently couched in the language of law. For example, the Special Powers Act, an 'emergency legislation' bill from 1922, formed the basis of the policy of internment (Guelke, 1991: 150). Within this legal context, the British authorities had great liberties in deciding when extrajudicial powers were necessary and needed to be activated, severely challenging any rule of law in Northern Ireland. It begs the question whether such *extra*judicial powers had simply become judicial, establishing a new normality outside the bounds of due process in which the executive unilaterally decided its own power with few, if any, legal checks and balances.

To this end, it is important to note that the suspension of internees' legal rights was itself formally legal. As Lowry reminds us, the extrajudicial confinement in Northern Ireland was an entirely lawful instrument of national policy, repeatedly affirmed by standard procedures in the British legislature and announced publicly and openly (1976: 170). The question is therefore not whether internment was *legal* in the conflict in Northern Ireland, but rather if it is a proper course for the law to pursue in a more fundamental sense. As Walsh forcefully states,

> The concept of an arrest power which permits the detention of a person without charge for an unlimited period merely on the subjective suspicion that he or she poses a threat to public order is a total negation of the law and the hallmark of a totalitarian state which pays scant regard to the basic principles of legality.
>
> (2000: 45)

As we discuss next, such a process subverts the generally positively accepted notion of a rule of law by turning it into rule by law, which is essentially a form of state lawfare.

From a human rights perspective, detention without trial, or internment, is both serious and notorious, giving rise to several legal difficulties (Dickson, 2009: 930). Crucially, the detainees in Ireland were seen as combatants in a domestic war, and as such terrorists, both the UK government and the ECHR were willing to dispense with some elements of fundamental rule of law to combat them. This turned a violent political conflict into a judicial quagmire, and this judicialisation subsequently paved the road for a further militarisation of the conflict.

Smith asserts that while internment was not a military necessity, it was a logical extension of the British government's military security approach to the conflict in Northern Ireland (2011). This approach undermined more moderate Republican voices and reinforced violent groups such as the IRA (ibid.: 152). State lawfare can in this case be taken quite literally; the judicialisation of the conflict was a means to further militarisation, rendering citizens possible combatants by removing their fundamental civil legal rights. In efforts to suppress political violence and assert the authority of the state, British authorities resorted to coercive measures including curfews, arbitrary house searches, and most notably, internment. This turned citizens from being subjects of the law, making them instead subject *to* law. If the goal was to turn Northern Ireland into a warzone where the military could successfully deploy in a manner they were accustomed to without the constraints of the rule of law, the strategy of lawfare certainly worked. Such measures were, however, demonstrably counterproductive in resolving the conflict. Moreover, they came at great political and judicial cost.

4.4.3 Implications

Just as the domestic lawfare analysed in the previous chapter, practices of state lawfare can lead to an erosion of fundamental legal rights in liberal democratic polities. Beyond the escalation of the very conflict which the policy of internment was designed to solve, internment also had serious long-term ramifications for legal rights and due process in Northern Ireland.

The extension of extrajudicial powers was seemingly exported to other parts of British society, with the British Army prerogative to search anyone in Northern Ireland whom they suspected of wrongdoings without a permit becoming a part of the Terrorism Act 2000, and authorised for the whole of London (Dickson, 2009: 962). The 28 days of pre-charge detention allowed by the Protection of Freedoms Act 2012 is also arguably a modern form of internment (Hayes, 2012: 128). Similarly, the CIA used the aforementioned 1978 ECHR ruling that the 'inhuman and degrading' treatment of Northern Irish detainees did not amount to torture as explicit legal backing for their interrogation practices in the infamous 'torture memos' (Corrigan, 2014). Later, both the US and UK would use the 'five techniques' first tested in Northern Ireland in war contexts such as Iraq and Afghanistan.

In Northern Ireland, the internment policy and the use of state lawfare initiatives to support a military security solution seemingly aggravated the territorial conflict. This had serious negative consequences not only for the conflict itself, but for the rule of law in the whole of the UK and for the extensive use of further extrajudicial powers in later conflicts such as the 'War on Terror' (Hayes, 2012: 128). Crucially, the solution to the conflict in Northern Ireland came not from state lawfare or militarisation, but from political compromise: the 1998 Good Friday Agreement, a legally binding bilateral treaty between the UK and the Republic of Ireland, recognises the right of self-determination for Northern Irish citizens. This is clearly specified in the first article of the agreement which stipulates that 'the legitimacy of whatever choice is freely exercised by a majority of the people of Northern Ireland with regard to its status, whether they prefer to continue to support the Union with Great Britain or a sovereign united Ireland' (Northern Ireland Office, 1998: 3). As we stated in the introduction, such 'secession clauses' are exceedingly rare and speaks to the UK government's willingness to compromise the unity of the state in the name of peace.

4.5 State lawfare in the Basque Country

In Spain, state lawfare is closely connected to the territorial challenges the central government faces in both the Basque Country and Catalonia. In the Basque Country, as in Northern Ireland, the aims of state lawfare were two-fold: dealing with the threat of political violence and addressing a territorial challenge.

The lawfare practised by the Spanish state in the Basque Country is instructive because of several factors: first, it involves a territorial conflict in which two sides, the majority government and a minority group, lay claim to the same territory, each considering the other to be illegitimate and unlawful. Second, it involves actual armed conflict as well, making it a multilevel conflict with distinct, parallel arenas and strategic action paths both political and violent. Third, the conflict involves state lawfare practised by first an autocratic state, the Fascist Spanish dictatorship, followed by a state in transition, and lastly a democratic state, the current Spanish polity. Each 'phase' had distinct opportunities and constraints in dealing with the situation and approached them differently.

This section will primarily focus on the latter. Like in the Northern Irish case scrutinised earlier, Spanish state territorial lawfare in the Basque Country was implemented in a context of secessionist violence, which in turn serves as a pretext to justify exceptional lawfare measures. However, Spanish state lawfare instruments in the Basque Country arguably went further than those applied by the UK in Northern Ireland, namely banning political parties and geographically dispersing jailed militants. For these reasons, the Basque Country is an excellent case study for a deeper understanding of state lawfare in internal territorial conflicts.

4.5.1 Situation

The illegalisation of parties in Spain has three distinct phases corresponding to the political contexts of Spain: Francoist dictatorship,

Transition, and full-fledged democracy. Only one party was allowed during Francoism; the Spanish Falange and the Spanish Transition to democracy enabled the formation of parties. However, not all parties were allowed to run for the first, pre-constitutional elections; the Spanish Ministry of the Interior did not allow the current government party in Catalonia, the pro-independence Republican Left of Catalonia (ERC), to participate (Castellanos López, 2016: 225; Hau, 2019).

Article 6 in the Spanish constitution and law 54/1978 on political parties surreptitiously opened the door for the banning of parties which were not 'democratic in their internal structure and functioning' or which had 'illicit associations' (BOE, 1978a, 1978b). This law, as the rest of the constitution, was negotiated during a period of fundamental uncertainty about the ultimate outcome of the democratisation process in Spain (Moroska-Bonkiewicz and Bourne, 2020: 470). Contemporary critics, which included precisely the left-wing and secessionist politicians previously banned during the dictatorship, argued the indeterminacy of the term 'internally democratic' would serve as an excuse to ban parties (ibid.).

More far-reaching was the controversial Law 6/2002 Party Law, which effectively banned radical Basque pro-independence parties such as Herri Batasuna and its successors due to alleged ties with ETA from 2003 to 2011. Here, courts were permitted to dissolve parties that 'violated democratic principles in a repeated and grave form, or aimed to undermine or destroy the regime of liberties, or injure or eliminate the democratic system' (BOE, 2002). As Moroska-Bonkiewicz and Bourne point out, the law was widely seen as a pretext for banning radical Basque nationalist parties (2020: 472), making it a clear case of a hegemonic, central state actor's use of state lawfare to 'solve' internal territorial conflicts.

The Spanish state lawfare in the Basque Country must be understood in the context of the successive Spanish government's attempts to quell secessionist armed violence and terrorism. Between 1962 and 2011, the Basque armed group ETA engaged in a campaign of political violence with the primary aim of establishing an independent Basque state and was directly responsible for the assassination of over 800 people (Castan Pinos and Radil, 2020: 1038). The political party 'Herri Batasuna' and its successors allegedly cooperated with ETA, operating as their 'political wing' (Justice, 2005; Cram, 2008). The most salient state lawfare measures pursued by Spain were targeted at this political or non-violent wing of the movement. Chief among these was the banning of Batasuna (Bourne, 2015).

4.5.2 Analysis

As Bourne notes, party bans are generally seen as the most militant, intolerant, or repressive measure to be deployed against anti-system parties or movements, and therefore the riskiest in terms of damage to the democratic system (2018: 23). This is the case since the political model of liberal, representative democracy is founded on promoting free competition between political projects, peaceful resolution of political conflicts, and civil society solutions, with the state being seen as an illegitimate arbiter in the selection among political projects (ibid.).

The banning of Batasuna was part of a wider strategy to dismantle what the Spanish Ministry of Interior typically referred to as 'ETA's network' (see Spanish Ministry of Interior, 2003). This strategy has been criticised for criminalising non-violent activists and for reducing a complex political problem to the simplistic conclusion of 'everything is ETA' (Batista, 2012). The strategy was accompanied by a panoply of parallel lawfare initiatives aimed at dismantling the political (non-violent) wing of the movement.

Unsurprisingly, the courts, in particular the Audiencia Nacional, were at the very centre of the strategy. This is illustrated by the several legal processes initiated by the Audiencia Nacional to indict a wide range of more than 170 individuals (Whitfield, 2014) and numerous organisations. This led to the arrests on charges of terrorism of newspaper editors (the newspaper *Egunkaria* was forced to close down), prisoners' support groups, civil society organisations, as well as environmentalist and pacifist groups (Amnesty, 2009; Whitfield, 2014; Bourne, 2015). Amnesty International warned that the strict interpretation of the concept of 'collaboration' with a terrorist organisation by Spanish courts could lead to the criminalisation 'of individuals who, by non-violent means, advocate greater autonomy of the Basque Country' (2009).

Additionally, with the aim of internationally isolating the party, in 2003, the Spanish government succeeded (after months of lobbying) at placing Batasuna on the EU and US terror lists (see Official Journal of the European Union, 2009). This move, which put on the same level individuals involved in violence with elected representatives (who ironically were still allowed to sit in the regional parliament), had crucial legal consequences for the party in terms of freezing of their financial assets, being subjected to international policing and, of course, de-legitimation. To put this into perspective, this effectively meant that the thousands of members of the party were members of a terrorist organisation and their cadre leaders of a terrorist organisation.

The Spanish central government used other repressive forms of state lawfare to combat the militant wing of the movement, ETA. One of the most important legal measures was the dispersal of prisoners. ETA's growing prison population became a focal point for propaganda and a politicisation of the struggle against the Spanish state, as well as playing a central role in ETA's internal ideological and doctrinal outlook (Warnes and Hannah, 2008). To deal with this issue, the Spanish authorities started in 1989 to desegregate and fragment ETA's prison network by dispersing their ETA prisoners, who had previously all been held in prisons in the Basque region, into small groups throughout the Spanish prison system (Alonso, 2011; Whitfield, 2014). This dispersal did fragment the internal cohesion of the ETA prison network but caused immense resentment amongst family members who had major problems visiting prisoners and led to highly publicised hunger strikes which allowed ETA a propaganda opportunity (Warnes and Hannah, 2008).

The dispersal policy has been condemned by Amnesty International and criticised for being one of the main hindrances to successful peace talks with ETA as it creates serious long-term grievances (Woodworth, 2007: 71). Similarly, the so-called Parot doctrine refers to a 2006 decision by the Spanish Supreme Court to deny convicted ETA militants specific rights that are granted by the 1973 Criminal Code that limit the maximum prison term to 30 years. This allowed for special, compound sentences of up to 5,000 years for convicted ETA members. This doctrine was, however, condemned and struck down by the ECHR in 2013 (ECHR, 2013). ETA convicts are also subject to an exceptional regime (FIES[4] regime), with extended periods of isolation, lack of access to the prison yard and unsupervised visits, and censorship of all prisoner correspondence, criticised by the Human Rights Watch (Ciocchini and Khoury, 2012: 188).

As a whole, the Spanish central state strategy for dealing with ETA, regardless of which party was in power, has focused on harsh judicial manoeuvres with the full cooperation of a willing judiciary.

4.5.3 Implications

The most significant and direct implication of the banning of Batasuna is that the party was unable to contest several elections in the period from 2003 to 2011. In the 2005 regional elections, the movement presented a proxy list that was eventually illegalised. In 2009, their exclusion from the regional elections (which they boycotted) had serious electoral consequences: for the first (and last) time, pro-Spanish parties had a majority in the Basque parliament which led to the first non-Basque nationalist regional president. After renouncing violence, Batasuna successors were able to contest the local elections with a wide pro-independence coalition (Bildu) in May 2011, obtaining 26% of the ballots (Basque Government, 2011). Said coalition has become the second most voted party in every Basque regional election since.

By illegalising Batasuna and its successors through state lawfare instruments, central Spanish governments attempted to remove the political avenue for the Basque pro-independence movement. This meant Batasuna was classified as unworthy of the rights granted to democratic parties. This strategy could have led to an escalation of the conflict by empowering hardline militants. However, it did not. Despite the weakness of the political leadership during the illegalisation period, the moderates within the movement were able to question ETA's leadership and 'impose' their unilateral peace process strategy, ultimately precipitating the end of ETA[5] (Barreiro and Sánchez-Cuenca, 2012; Murua, 2017).

More generally, while the illegalisation of parties may bring short-term gain in terms of weakening a separatist movement, it can also erode trust in the central government in the territories where secession movements operate. Ciocchini and Khoury argue Spain engages in 'illegal legality', paradoxically violating human rights through the lawful enforcement of law constructed as democratic measures of counterterrorism (2012: 179). Such measures may exacerbate and prolong conflict in the long run, harm the central government legitimacy, and make political compromise even more difficult. It also ensures that there will be continued grievances in the population which secessionist parties can mobilise.

This is the case for even moderate dissidents; for 20 years between 1990 and 2010, the Basque government refused to challenge any state law or regulation before the Spanish Constitutional Court due to a lack of trust in the court's impartiality (Arzoz, 2018: 50). Since state lawfare does not resolve the fundamental political differences behind a territorial conflict, its long-term efficacy is questionable. As Bourne notes, party bans merely address the symptom of anti-system support, while long-term strategies that, for example engage civil society can address the root causes of discontent (2018: 37).

Similar to the UK government's strategy in Northern Ireland analysed previously, the Spanish central government's approach to Batasuna was closely linked to a process of securitisation (ibid.: 38), where a political issue is presented as posing an existential security threat to the state (Wæver, 1993; Buzan *et al.*, 1998). Effectively, state lawfare, such as party bans, removes political solutions but does not remove politics itself from a given conflict. Further, in the case of secessionist conflicts, since *all* pro-independence political parties represent an existential threat to the state and constitution in theory, this would give central governments an unsustainably broad pretext for illegalisation. The problematic question is whether pursuing the same objectives (independent statehood) as extremist, violent groups is itself sufficient to create a link between a given party or candidate and such terrorist groups (Bale, 2014: 211). This danger of 'guilt by association' was, in fact, raised in the Spanish case by a UN Special Rapporteur and remains particularly pertinent in the Basque case (ibid.). All these issues question both the moral and judicial legitimacy as well as the efficacy of lawfare when used by central governments in state territorial conflicts.

4.6 State lawfare in Catalonia

As Brown Swan and Cetrà argue, when it comes to Catalonia, successive Spanish governments have equated law enforcement with democracy, adopting a legalistic approach to dealing with political dissent and territorial struggles in stark contrast to, for example the UK (2020: 54). Indeed, the Spanish government's 'insurmountable legal obstacles' for Catalonia (Dardanelli and Mitchell, 2014: 102) appear to frame the independence issue as being about law abidance and illegality, neglecting fundamental questions about democracy, belonging, sovereignty, and federalism that the territorial conflict likewise raises. These factors all make the Spanish government's handling of the territorial conflict in Catalonia a compelling case for studying an emergent form of state lawfare.

4.6.1 Situation

The recent 'Catalan crisis' culminated with the unilateral independence referendum in October 2017 (Humlebæk and Hau, 2020). Unlike in Northern Ireland and the Basque Country, the Catalan conflict did not involve political violence. However, the Spanish central government actively engaged in state lawfare to curtail the pro-independence movement in Catalonia and safeguard Spain's territorial integrity.

From 2012 to 2017, successive Catalan governments, encouraged by large civil society organisations, pursued initiatives and policies aimed at self-determination and secession (Castan Pinos and Sacramento, 2019). The Spanish government responded to this challenge with a strategy primarily based on the judicialisation of the Catalan conflict, attempting to reduce inherently political issues to matters of public order and legality. This strategy was consistently supported by the two largest Spanish political parties. Former Spanish Vice-President Soraya Sáenz de Santamaría from the conservative Partido Popular, for example repeatedly argued that 'there is no democracy beyond the law'. Similarly, current Vice-President Carmen Calvo, from the social democratic party PSOE, has made it clear that 'we cannot talk about what is not legal' (cited in Brown Swan and Cetrà, 2020: 54).

As a direct response to the situation in Catalonia, the organic law of the Constitutional Court was amended in October 2015 solely with the votes of the governing, conservative PP party to provide the Court with extended executive powers including the temporary replacement of any public official in noncompliance with the Court's rulings (Arzoz, 2018: 69). The Court declared its new powers to be consistent with the Constitution and used them for the first time to enforce a prohibition of the Catalan independence referendum on 1 October 2017 (Spanish Constitutional Court, 2017).

The most visible evidence of the state lawfare strategy in Catalonia was the incarceration of several political and civil society leaders. In October 2019, nine high-ranking Catalan politicians and civil society leaders were found guilty of the crime of 'sedition' and given prison sentences ranging from nine to 13 years for organising the 2017 referendum on Catalan independence. These harsh sentences have reopened debates about the judicialisation of political problems and the alleged ideological bias of the Spanish judiciary. The United Nations Working Group on Arbitrary Detention urged Spain to release the Catalan leaders and investigate their 'arbitrary detention', which in their view is 'in contravention of . . . the Universal Declaration of Human Rights' (Human Rights Council, 2019: 16). In the same vein, a report by Fernand de Varennes, UN Special Rapporteur on minority issues to the Human Rights Council, 'expressed grave concerns' regarding the criminal charges against Catalan leaders, urging Spain to review its legal definition of sedition as '[N]on-violent political

dissent by minorities should not give rise . . . to criminal charges'
(Human Rights Council, 2020: 14). All Catalan prisoners were eventually released from prison after the Spanish government approved a
pardon in June 2021, with the stipulation that they could not hold
public office for the duration of their sentence.

4.6.2 Analysis

A cardinal question in the analysis of Spanish state lawfare is whether
the imprisoned Catalan leaders were 'political prisoners'. If, as Spanish
left-wing groups and the Catalan independence supporters argue, there
are political prisoners in Spain, this would be a serious injury to the
health of Spanish democracy. Yet the majority of Spanish political parties
and central state actors flatly deny that the Catalan leaders were political prisoners, insisting the imprisonment was a purely legal procedure
devoid of any politics whatsoever. Such a legalist semantic approach has
some shortcomings, however. By this logic, there are no political prisoners anywhere in the world, nor can there be. There is no state, at least not
a liberal democratic one, that officially accepts having political prisoners,
since there is always an article of the criminal code that guarantees their
persecution according to the law. Any jailing of a politician or activist
for political actions will have a legal ground, even if it merely constitutes
a pretext, and will necessarily remain a political question.

This is evidenced by the Parliamentary Assembly of the Council
of Europe's tautological set of criteria for who can be considered a
'political prisoner' as someone detained for 'purely political reasons'
or if the legal proceedings involve the detainee being 'clearly unfair
and appears to be connected with political motives of the authorities' (PACE, 2012). Essentially, the debate about political prisoners is a
political discussion, not a matter of legality. This is especially the case in
Catalonia, where the relevant crime was 'sedition' and (violent) rebellion against the state. Lawyer and policymaker for the *Unidas Podemos*
party, Jaume Asens, pointed out that the indictment against Catalan
leaders was highly problematic since the crimes of sedition and rebellion are ill-defined within the Spanish legal system and have no precedent in democratic Spain. In an unflattering historical parallel, Asens
asserted that these very same crimes were used extensively to punish
anti-Francoist dissidents when the regime had trouble defining a precise offence but still wanted to enact punishment (2017).

Drawing on Machiavelli, Holmes argues that governing actors
will seek to outsource punishment to other state apparatuses while

retaining the power to pardon, since this is more beneficial in gaining political power (2003: 28). This was exactly the rationale behind the Spanish state's legal crackdown on the Catalan independence movement following the non-agreed referendum in 2017. The judiciary was put in charge of 'solving' the political antagonism between pro-secession actors and the central state. Proposals for a political solution were rejected by Prime Minister Sánchez as he labelled it a purely judicial issue. However, Sánchez reserved the power to pardon the Catalan leaders, doing so already in June 2021 against the public criticism of the Supreme Court – with the caveat that they could not hold political office. Similarly, although Sánchez emphasised the separation of powers and his lack of control over the Supreme Court in the sentencing of Catalan leaders, this was not the case when he vowed to overturn a Supreme Court ruling on controversial mortgage fees (see Cué, 2018). This means that central state actors appear to be flexible in their understanding of what is legal and what is political according to whether it serves their own interests.

Unlike in Northern Ireland and the Basque Country, the Catalan conflict has not involved political violence. However, Spanish state institutions used 'violence' as a key part of a securitisation discourse (Wæver, 1993), presenting the Catalan independence movement as an existential security threat. This rhetorical strategy was aimed at accomplishing a two-fold objective: to legitimise the state lawfare strategy of the government, and to de-legitimise Catalan policymakers and grassroots civil society activists by framing the pro-independence movement as 'violent'. As part of this strategy, the public prosecutor charged Catalan policymakers and social activists respectively with crimes of 'rebellion' and 'terrorism'.

'Rebellion' necessarily involves violence according to the definitions of the Spanish penal code (BOE, 1995), making the legal argument for this charge untenable due to the nonexistent evidence of political violence in Catalonia.[6] In parallel, the Public Prosecutor, the Guardia Civil, and Spanish centralist parties attempted to frame actions of peaceful civil disobedience as 'terrorism' in order to fit the charges (Brew, 2018). In a notable case, pro-independence activist Tamara Carrasco called for a demonstration to block Barcelona's port in a Whatsapp group and was charged with terrorism.[7] She spent 18 months under house arrest during a prolonged investigation in the Audiencia Nacional that eventually yielded no proof of a crime[8] (Altimira, 2020). Effectively, such serious accusations allow the judiciary to exact pre-trial punishment through detentions and house arrests, even when the accused is eventually acquitted. This makes it a powerful lawfare deterrent against challenging the territorial status quo.

4.6.3 Implications

Insofar as it does not compel pro-union Spanish parties to articulate a clear case for staying together, the Spanish state lawfare potentially harms both the territorial debate in Spain and the instrumental possibility for building compromise, finding common ground, and creating new solutions to difficult political issues. Since the central state is inevitably governed by majority nation parties, minority secessionist parties effectively have little to no influence on Spanish laws and are incapable of effecting the necessary constitutional reforms that would allow for a self-determination referendum.

While the secessionist movements are criticised for not upholding the (Spanish) law, the legitimacy of which they fundamentally oppose, shifting majority party governments have bent it to their political will in service of the central state, rather than engaging in political compromise with the pro-self secession actors that threaten the nominal unity of Spain. Further, minority parties have no legal recourse to prevent central state lawfare, such as the application of Article 155 of the Spanish Constitution which allows the central government to 'restore constitutional order'. This article was used to suspend Catalan regional autonomy and dissolve the democratically elected Catalan Parliament following the unilateral independence referendum in 2017. The application of this article also shows that from the central state's point of view, the regional autonomy in the Spanish system is a privilege rather than a right and can be revoked as 'punishment' in times of territorial political conflict. Former Spanish Constitutional Court lawyer Joaquín Urías argues that Article 155 is not merely a state coercion mechanism but a 'conflict resolution' political instrument that empowers the Spanish central government to impose its will over a noncompliant region (2019: 112), and he has criticised presenting the conflict in Catalonia as a legal problem to be solved by judges (Urías Martínez, 2020).

The Spanish government's use of state lawfare in Catalonia and the application of Article 155 has not only had serious consequences for the centre–periphery cleavage in Spain, but it also raised questions about the quality of Spain's liberal democracy as a whole (Gagnon, 2020: 87). A recent study by the *Economist* relegated Spain from being classified from a 'full democracy' to a 'flawed democracy' following ongoing political divisions over the appointment of new magistrates to the General Council of the Judiciary, the body that oversees the judicial system and is intended to guarantee its independence (EIU, 2022: 10).

Spain also came close to being reclassified as a 'flawed democracy' after its score fell in 2017 in the aftermath of the Catalan referendum crisis, and the central Madrid government's aforementioned legal repressions against pro-independence Catalan politicians for acting unconstitutionally. Similarly, Spain is among the four EU countries where citizens have the lowest perception about judicial independence (European Commission, 2019), speaking to a serious lack of credibility for the judiciary. Pundits such as Mezey have criticised Spain's use of repressive powers of the state such as 'police, prison, and the heavy hand of criminal law' (2019) to hamstring the Catalan independence movement, essentially fueling the flames of secessionism through state lawfare. Others, such as Urías, have raised questions about the political leanings of the judiciary and criticised the use of convictions without appeal and provisional detentions in Catalonia to remove 'any possibility of a political answer by the independentists' (2020).

Despite these costs, Spanish state lawfare has managed to contain the Catalan crisis. Partly, this was achieved by inducing fear amongst secessionist policymakers and pro-independence activists with the clear message that challenging the territorial unity of the state would be punished severely. Moreover, another key achievement of state lawfare in this case was the transformation of the secessionists' rhetorical frame. Following the imprisonment of politicians and activists in November 2017, this shifted from demands of independence to focusing primarily on grievances related to anti-repressive measures. Since the restoration of Catalan autonomy in June 2018, successive pro-independence Catalan governments have not pursued a single action nor attempted to pass any piece of pro-secessionist legislation.

In sum, the judicialisation of the political-territorial issue in Catalonia bears the hallmarks of arbitrary application of law and does not constitute a political solution to the conflict. Although the use of state lawfare to deal with the Catalan crisis has proven brutally effective in the short run and may help centralist parties to win elections, it weakens the possibility for long-term settlements due to furthering grievances between political opponents. It also has the possibility to seriously damage the democratic credibility of Spain, making it a costly practice in spite of the considerable short-term gains involved.

4.7 Conclusion

As the Comaroffs write, legal instruments appear to offer a ready means of commensuration between heterodox understandings of belonging and political subjectivities (2006). The underlying assumption is that communal loyalties competing with that of the state majority, such as in the case of territorial minorities, are inherently liable to disorder, criminality, violence – and dangerous difference. This challenges the modernist nation-state ideal of the imagined community (cf. Anderson, 1991), a commitment to the fiction of cultural, linguistic, and sometimes ethnic homogeneity and often violently upheld. In Catalonia, state lawfare pursued by Spain through the increasingly harsh judicial verdicts on inherently political issues is driven by a fundamental, existential battle for the perceived homogeneity and territorial order of Spain.

In the Basque Country and Northern Ireland, state lawfare conducted by Spain and the UK respectively bears the hallmarks of securitisation with the legal and moral conundrums of counter-terrorism added to conflicting ethnoterritorial disputes. The territorial dispossession of Native Americans during the US westward expansion asks fundamental questions of citizens' equality before the law, judicial racialisation, and the constitutional dehumanisation of minorities. These cases are all complex, multifaceted conflicts requiring a host of solutions and cannot be solved solely via the heavy hand of the law and arbitrary judicial decisions.

The modernist nation-state has been grounded in a culture of legality from its very beginning, its spirit being 'the spirit of the law' (Comaroff and Comaroff, 2007: 140). In composite nation-states with pervasive territorial and national conflicts, there appears to be an almost irreducible difference. The language of law and legalism presents itself as an ostensibly neutral medium for people of difference – belonging to different nations, social classes, material circumstances, different identities – to deal with conflicts. However, when powerful, central state actors resort to state lawfare in the hopes of creating order and resolving deep-seated cleavages, they are attempting to rely on supposedly universal standards to negotiate fundamental, political differences. This forges false impressions of consonance and harmony that do not represent the underlying, conflict-ridden reality involved in political compromise.

When ruling on the unconstitutionality of for example a referendum on independence such as the unilateral Catalan plebiscite in

2017, judges will be forced to engage in fundamental jurisprudence and reflect upon the very philosophy of law, national unity, and right and wrong. This includes considerations of free speech or the right to assembly for independence-seeking minority groups, which necessarily go against the majority nation's opinion. Fundamental debates about the future of a polity requires courts to not only follow laws, but to make them, and this process is highly susceptible to acts of lawfare if the judicial and political systems are not sufficiently safeguarded from it.

Having analysed the applications and implications of state lawfare in internal territorial conflicts, we now move on to a radically different variant, that of lawfare from below pursued by civil society and 'weak' actors.

Notes

1 As the UK has an uncodified Constitution, this is technically not a constitutionally enshrined right but has a similar, constitutive character.
2 'The Congress shall have power to dispose of and make all needful rules and regulations respecting the territory or other property belonging to the United States' (US Constitution, 1787).
3 A Council of Europe special body that was in charge of evaluating the admissibility of cases related to human rights. It operated between 1954 and 1988.
4 FIES stands for 'Ficheros de internos de especial seguimiento', that is Files of Inmates Under Special Surveillance.
5 Weakened by successful police operations and under pressure from the moderates within the movement, ETA announced the end of its 'armed campaign' in 2011 (ETA, 2011) and the 'complete dissolution of its structures' in 2018 (ETA, 2018).
6 Arguably, the main instance of violence occurred on 1 October 2017, when the Spanish national police and the paramilitary Guardia Civil attempted to prevent the non-agreed referendum using coercive state violence, injuring 1,066 voters (BBC, 2017b).
7 The charges were made possible by a controversial redefinition of 'terrorism' penalising remarks made on social media, which was enacted by the conservative PP government in 2015 and criticised by Amnesty for severely curtailing freedom of expression in Spain (Amnesty International, 2022).
8 The public prosecutor's explicit reasoning was that a large demonstration in a public place of transit such as a port or an airport would inevitably lead to violence as 'the security forces of the State guarding such installations are necessarily going to react' (Altimira, 2021).

Chapter 5

Asymmetric lawfare
A weapon of the weak

5.1 Introduction

This chapter focuses on an important dimension: lawfare conducted by non-hegemonic actors, which we define as 'asymmetric lawfare'. The chapter shows that although lawfare is generally associated with powerful actors (particularly states), as we have shown in previous chapters, hegemonic actors do not have exclusive rights over the practice. Both small, 'weak' states and non-state actors such as civil society groups or Indigenous rights activists also resort to lawfare for a range of politically driven purposes. This type of lawfare has been characterised as a 'weapon of the weak' (Comaroff and Comaroff, 2006: 31) and as 'insurgent lawfare' (Comaroff and Comaroff, 2009: 57). The chapter primarily concentrates on the strategic use of legal instruments by 'weak' actors at either state or international levels.

Central to asymmetrical lawfare conducted by civil society actors is the principle of universal jurisdiction. In 2001, a group of leading scholars published the *Princeton Principles on Universal Jurisdiction*, defining this concept as

> criminal jurisdiction based solely on the nature of the crime, without regard to where the crime was committed, the nationality of the alleged or convicted perpetrator, the nationality of the victim, or any other connection to the state exercising such jurisdiction.
> (cited by University of Minnesota, 2001)

Needless to say, one of the great unresolved challenges associated with universal jurisdiction is its application and implementation. The European Court of Human Rights (ECHR), considered by some as one of the most successful examples of international justice (Wildhaber, 2004; Von Staden, 2018), has the significant limitation that its jurisdiction is

DOI: 10.4324/9781003289869-5

restricted to the members of the Council of Europe. Some of the cases analysed in this chapter will illustrate the difficulties that civil society organisations encounter to find legal venues to conduct lawfare.

Asymmetrical lawfare involves different courts, both national and transnational, and multiple actors of a very divergent nature. Frequently, asymmetric lawfare takes place in the 'global public domain', defined by Ruggie as 'an increasingly institutionalized transnational arena of discourse, contestation, and action . . . involving private as well as public actors' (2004: 504). States may, of course, play a role in this 'arena', but they are not necessarily central to it. In numerous cases, such as in the Ogoni conflict, legal battles take place primarily between civil society groups and transnational companies (TNCs).

TNCs are often targeted by states and civil society organisations through lawfare, which can have significant negative consequences for corporations. It is therefore not surprising that, as explained by Shamir, TNCs use strategies such as corporate social responsibility (CSR) to prevent civil society actors (or states) from using legal means against them (2004). However, it is not clear whether their active use of legal mechanisms, for example through litigations, constitutes lawfare. According to the definition we provided in Chapter 1, lawfare is a *multifaceted law-based instrument that can be used by a wide range of actors in both military as well as non-military contexts to pursue political objectives.*

With a few rare exceptions,[1] TNCs' use of legal means, both domestically and internationally, is aimed at defending their corporate interests, and therefore, their intent is not to 'pursue political interests' in *stricto sensu*. In a nutshell, the rationale is that when lobbying is not sufficient to influence lawmaking, corporations resort to more radical means to defend their commercial interests through litigation, effectively taking legal actions against regulators to recoup the losses stemming from unfavourable legislation (Ruggie, 2018: 323). Corporate litigation can be therefore seen as a continuation of (unsuccessful) lobbying. With this caveat in mind, we reiterate that we do not see these fundamentally commercial interests as political in nature and, therefore, we do not include further analysis of corporate legal strategies in this book.

Conversely, as we argue in the following section, legal mechanisms used by civil society actors lie squarely within the realm of politics and do constitute an instance of asymmetric lawfare.

5.2 Civil society lawfare

Prior to analysing how asymmetric lawfare is conducted by civil society actors, we must acknowledge that the use of the term lawfare in non-hegemonic contexts is not universally accepted. Handmaker, for instance, contends that there is a clear-cut distinction between lawfare and legal mobilisation (2019, 2020). This distinction is justified by the fact that the former, Handmaker argues, carries negative, illegitimate, and hegemonic connotations and, therefore, the legal instrumentalisation strategies of civic-led advocacy groups should be referred to as 'legal mobilisation' (2019: 10) instead. Dunlap, the aforementioned scholar credited with reframing the concept of lawfare, admits that it may be used with a pejorative connotation (2010). Additionally, using securitisation theory frames, Gordon points out that the use of the term lawfare in the specific context of human rights litigation is not descriptive but normative, having the specific purpose of reframing 'liberal human rights NGOs as a security threat' (2014: 312).

For various reasons, we, however, disagree with this view and argue that the term is perfectly valid to describe the legal strategies of civil society actors and social activists. As explained in Chapter 2, lawfare does not necessarily denote negative and illegitimate political actions and can be understood as a neutral instrument used by multiple actors to pursue their political interests. In some cases, lawfare might be used to undermine political opposition (see Chapter 3) or to consolidate the territorial status quo in national conflicts (Chapter 4), and in these cases the practice carries significant costs, not least in terms of democratic backsliding. In other contexts, however, asymmetric lawfare may be employed to challenge hegemonic actors by actors who have few resources and little or no chance of success using conventional means of resistance.

Moreover, a considerable number of authors scrutinising the legal mobilisation of non-hegemonic actors use the term lawfare when describing said phenomenon without ascribing pejorative connotations to the term (Comaroff and Comaroff, 2006; Randeria, 2007; Gloppen and St Clair, 2012; Joseph, 2012; Gloppen, 2018; Spector, 2019). In this regard, it is key to highlight the line of reasoning of Jean Comaroff and John Comaroff, who argued that while lawfare is primarily used by powerful actors, it can also 'sometimes' operate as 'a weapon of the weak, turning authority back on itself by commissioning the sanction of the court to make claims for resources, recognition, voice, integrity, sovereignty' (2006: 31).

It is nonetheless important to clarify that there are fundamental differences between the usage of lawfare by states, particularly great powers, and by civil society groups. While technically we are dealing with the same mechanism, the implementation, resources, rationale, and the political objectives of the practice differ considerably. Specifically, as we saw in previous chapters, states use lawfare in conjunction with a panoply of other methods to uphold, wield, and consolidate their power. Instead, civil society actors lack military means, instruments of economic coercion, etc. As this chapter will show, this fundamental difference regarding power asymmetry leads to fundamental implications, most notably in terms of efficacy and successfulness.

Specifically, the lack of coercive means that can be used in tandem with lawfare necessarily disempowers civil society actors vis-à-vis states, generating important power asymmetries. Without force to back up their lawfare efforts, at the very most, the use of lawfare by social movements or civil society groups can be coordinated with traditional protest instruments such as street mobilisations, direct actions, and, depending on the resources of the actors involved, a PR or social media campaign. This underpins Randeria's argument that social movements are increasingly conducting their traditional methods of political participation 'in tandem with court litigation in the national and international arena' (2007: 39).

This vital point leads us to the concept of 'legal mobilisation', which has been used to conceptualise social movements' tactical use of legal instruments (Burstein, 1991; Lehoucq and Taylor, 2020). In the view of Lehoucq and Taylor, social movements across the world 'have increasingly incorporated legal strategies into their repertoires of contention' (2020: 166). In many cases, lawfare is the last option civil society organisations resort to in the pursuit of their political interests. Here it represents a form of activism used to confront a far more powerful adversary in the context of an asymmetrical conflict, typically a state, a transnational corporation or both. Lawfare, after all, has often been perceived as an instrument of the weak (e.g., US Department of Defense, 2005; Rishikof, 2008).

While asymmetrical lawfare has been far less scrutinised than the other dimensions covered in previous chapters, there is a small but growing body of literature that addresses the practice. In that regard, Siri Gloppen's definition of lawfare as 'the strategic use of rights, law and litigation by actors of different breeds to advance contested political and social goals' (2018: 6) appears particularly relevant. This definition widens the scope of the term, enabling a scrutiny of a myriad of societal conflicts, including rights-based activism, through the prism of lawfare, or as Gloppen puts it, 'lawfare from below' (ibid.).

In recent years, numerous empirical studies have focused on specific cases of 'social' or bottom up lawfare, where non-hegemonic actors engage in the practice as a vehicle to pursue a variety of goals (Fay,

2013; Gloppen and St Clair, 2012; Joseph, 2012; Spector, 2019). One of the most common areas where weak actors use lawfare is environmentalism. To this end, the concept 'green lawfare' was coined by Australian policymakers in 2015 to denounce the litigation by civil society environmentalist groups who used federal courts to prevent the opening of a coal mine in Northeastern Australia (Clark, 2016; Konkes, 2018). In the view of Australia's former Attorney-General and Senator, George Brandis, green lawfare was nothing short of 'vigilante litigation' conducted 'by people whose aim is to game the system, who have no legitimate interest other than to prosecute a political vendetta against development' (cited by Potter, 2015). As explained earlier, lawfare is often associated with pejorative connotations that denote illegitimate law-based strategies.

Understood broadly, however, green lawfare includes a wide array of activist-driven uses of legal instruments aimed at safeguarding the environment. This is hardly surprising as, increasingly, political disputes are settled in legal arenas. Environmental issues are not an exception. As put by Konkes, '[T]he law and the courts have long been a part of environmental campaign strategies' (2018: 200). The extensive use of this practice in multiple countries has led to what some have described as the 'global judicialization' of environmental politics and disputes (Vanhala, 2012; Kramarz et al., 2017).

The branch of green lawfare specifically addressing climate change issues is commonly known as 'climate change litigation' (Lin, 2012; Vallejo and Gloppen, 2013; Peel and Lin, 2019; Setzer and Vanhala, 2019), though Gloppen and St Clair explicitly refer to it as 'climate change lawfare' (2012). In their view, the rationale of this type of lawfare is to attempt to change international regulation regimes and governmental policies so that they prioritise 'climate change mitigation and adaptation' (Gloppen and St Clair, 2012: 909). Similarly, Lin views climate change litigation as the way in which to 'use legal avenues to hold certain entities accountable for their contribution to global warming' (2012: 57).

These 'legal avenues' are becoming tremendously popular and increasingly successful[2] (Setzer and Higham, 2021). This is partly to do with the 2015 Paris Agreement, an international treaty based on non-legally binding 'national mitigation pledges' (Falkner, 2016: 1124), whose main aim is to limit the global 'temperature increase to 1.5°C above pre-industrial levels' (United Nations, 2015: 3). Despite its non-legally binding character, the Paris Agreement triggered 'an explosion' of 'national climate change legislation' (Eskander et al., 2021: 69) as well as a reinvigoration of climate change litigation (Setzer and Van-hala, 2019). This reinvigoration is supported by empirical evidence. According to a recent report from the London School of Economics, in 2021, there were 1,841 ongoing cases of climate change litigation worldwide, the vast majority of which (75%) were filed in the US (Setzer and Higham, 2021).

While climate change lawfare is a relatively new phenomenon, human rights lawfare, or human rights litigation, has played a prominent role for various decades. Civil society organisations across the world have been using legal mechanisms to uphold human rights and denouncing human rights violations committed by both states and TNCs, both in national and international courts. As a result, organisations such as Amnesty International or Human Rights Watch have been credited for shaping human rights law as well as 'the law of armed conflict' (Kittrie, 2016: 46). It is important to note that human rights lawfare does not exclusively take place in military conflicts and can also emerge in cases without actual warfare. This is illustrated, for instance by the cases brought by civil society organisations against international corporations for their (alleged) role in human rights violations. While these types of cases have exponentially grown in recent decades, the vast majority of them end up being dismissed, putting their efficacy somewhat in doubt (Schrempf-Stirling and Wettstein, 2017).

Central to the discussion of asymmetric lawfare, particularly in the realm of human rights, is the aforementioned concept of universal jurisdiction. The debates around the legitimacy and validity of such universality applied to human rights were reanimated in the late 1990s (see Kissinger, 2001; Roth, 2001) in the wake of the establishment of the International Criminal Court (ICC[3]). The arrest of late Chilean dictator Augusto Pinochet in 1998 following a warrant by Spanish judge Baltasar Garzón, has been heralded as a 'model[4] of universal jurisdiction where extraterritorial prosecution is justified on the grounds that 'grave [human right] offenses concern all members of the international legal community' (Wedgwood, 1999: 834).

5.3 Civil society lawfare: cases

Our empirical section focuses on cases of asymmetric lawfare where environmental and human rights legal activism intersect, in a relationship that is increasingly symbiotic. As Savaresi and Auz point out, 'human rights arguments are increasingly used in climate change lawsuits' (2019: 245). One of the examples where these two dimensions clearly conflate is the litigation battles between a transnational company, Chevron, and Indigenous groups in the Amazon, where the latter tried to seek compensation for decades of environmental – and human rights – damage through court proceedings (Joseph, 2012). With the aim of shedding light on this intersection of various forms of civil society lawfare, the following paragraphs will analyse two legal cases involving environmentalism and human rights: the Ogoni conflict and the Dakota Access Pipeline.

5.3.1 The Ogoni case

The Ogoni case offers a clear illustration of human rights and environmentalist asymmetric lawfare launched to uphold the rights of underprivileged groups facing immensely more powerful adversaries: a state, Nigeria, and a transnational corporation, Shell. It represents a case of remedial lawfare, where activists resort to legal instruments and litigation in international courts to seek compensation for the violation of their human and environmental rights. A succinct analysis of the lawfare strategies by Ogoni civil society groups is, consequently, particularly pertinent for understanding asymmetric lawfare.

In 1992, Ken Saro-Wiwa, the leader of the Movement for the Survival of the Ogoni People (MOSOP), an environmentalist and human rights social movement, was imprisoned for several months without trial in Nigeria (Saro-Wiwa, 1995). The arrest of this highly popular and influential civil society leader represents a clear case of state lawfare, where the Nigerian government used coercive legal instruments to silence a non-violent opposition voice. In fact, Saro-Wiwa was a victim of the most extreme form of state lawfare. In 1995, following what was widely considered a sham trial (Pegg, 2000; Boele *et al.*, 2001), he, along with eight MOSOP activists, were sentenced to death[5] and subsequently hanged.

This case, which is known as the 'Ogoni 9', has ramifications which go well beyond the tragic consequences of governmental use of state lawfare. Saro-Wiwa and his fellow companions' struggle was first and foremost aimed at protecting the environment in their ancestral lands from oil exploitation carried out by Shell. Obi eloquently summarises the grievances that mobilised the MOSOP against this transnational oil company: 'Shell has expropriated peasant land, polluted the ecosystem and virtually destroyed the livelihood of the local Ogoni peasantry, without paying heed to initially peaceful demands for restitution' (1997: 138). MOSOP, like many other social movements, pursued different strategies to carry out its goals, including mass mobilisation through protests, awareness campaigns, cooperation with international civil society organisations (see Saro-Wiwa, 1995; MOSOP, 2015) and eventually bottom-up lawfare. The latter, which was primarily aimed at seeking justice for the murdered victims in international courts, provided some measure of success for the families of the Ogoni 9.

As we mentioned in the introduction to this chapter, a key aspect of civil society lawfare is universal jurisdiction, that is finding appropriate extraterritorial venues for legal action. As such, the first challenge of the Ogoni case was where to file the complaint and to determine which court would be competent to enact justice. The Centre for Constitutional Rights (CCR), which represented the relatives of the murdered activists, decided to file the lawsuits against Shell[6] for human rights abuses including 'crimes against humanity, in violation of customary international law' in a New York court (Southern District Court NY, 1996: 17). At first glance, this would seem peculiar, given that the alleged crimes did not involve the US: they were committed against Nigerian citizens in Nigeria, and the company sued was headquartered in the Netherlands.

Interestingly, the decision to bring the case to a US court is explained by a unique – and remarkably short – piece of US legislation from 1789, the Alien Tort Statute[7] (ATS), which arguably allows foreigners to file cases involving human rights abuses overseas in US district courts. There has been a legal and scholarly discussion debating whether the ATS paves the way for universal jurisdiction (see Burley, 1989; Ku, 2013). What is relevant for our case is that the Ogoni activists' legal team used this provision to file the lawsuits in the US. The long duration of the legal proceedings (from 1996 to 2009) is partly explained by the fact that Shell's defendants attempted to dismiss the lawsuits by arguing that the ATS was not applicable to the case (CCR, 2022), and therefore the court had no jurisdiction over it.

In a small victory for the Ogoni activists, the parties agreed on a settlement in 2009, and Shell compensated the victims with $15.5 million, albeit without admitting any wrongdoings (Mouawad, 2009). Such asymmetric lawfare is however not always successful, and a similar lawsuit filed by MOSOP activists in 2002, *Kiobel v. Royal Dutch Petroleum Co.* 2013, experienced a very different fate. The latter ended up at the US Supreme Court which concluded that there was 'no indication that the ATS was passed to make the United States a uniquely hospitable forum for the enforcement of international norms' (US Supreme Court, 2013: 3). For the Ogoni movement, this Supreme Court ruling represented a clear defeat of its lawfare strategy. More generally, the fact that the ATS does 'not provide a venue for justice' (CCR, 2018) has been interpreted as 'the surprising death of universal jurisdiction' (Ku, 2013: 835), at least, under the ATS.

The Ogoni case illustrates that while it is possible for civil society actors to engage in lawfare, it can be a long, tortuous task with uncertain outcomes. This is partly explained by the lack of international legal venues to enact justice in cases of human and environmental rights violations. Rather than being exceptional, these challenges and limitations are inherent to asymmetrical lawfare, which is by no means guaranteed to succeed, but which nonetheless enable 'weak' actors to, at least, attempt to challenge a much stronger political opponent.

5.3.2 The Dakota Access Pipeline protests

Another instructive case of civil society lawfare, or lawfare from below, is that of the Dakota Access Pipeline protests on Standing Rock Indian Reservation in North and South Dakota. Like the Ogoni people, this case is characterised by the intersection of environmental and Indigenous activism in favour of human and cultural rights.

The Dakota Access Pipeline (DAPL) protests,[8] which emerged in 2016, is a movement involving 300 Native nations and thousands of protesters against a new $3.8 billion pipeline carrying heavy crude oil across and to refineries in the Mexican Golf (Estes, 2017: 115). The activists, many of whom are from the Standing Rock Indian Reservation under whose land the pipeline runs, claim great risks to freshwater resources and the local environment. This led to the most broad-base Native American-led grassroots social movement campaign in US History (Steinman, 2019: 1070). The protests included physical actions, political lobbying, and crucially for this book, legal activism. The movement received formal encouragement by many Native American nations, support from Indigenous people from elsewhere in the Americas, and counted political allies such as presidential candidates Bernie Sanders and Jill Stein (ibid.).

The DAPL protests involved the peaceful occupation of the pipeline construction site in what Estes (2017) terms 'counter sovereignty', with Native American religious rituals as well as anti-capitalist and pro-environment speeches. The protests received global media coverage and created vast and powerful networks on social media that helped control the news narrative and sway political élites (Johnson, 2017: 159). Over 800 people were arrested between 2016 and 2017, since parts of the land on which protests were held fall under the technical jurisdiction of the Army Corps of Engineers in violation of the 1851 and 1868 Fort Laramie Treaties (ibid.: 120).

However, while the DAPL protests were culturally and politically significant, showcasing the strength of intersectional pro-environmental activism anchored in Native traditions, the true victories of the movement arguably did not emerge from direct action, but from bottom-up lawfare. This is epitomised by the Standing Rock Sioux nation lawsuit against the US Army Corps in 2016, claiming it violated multiple federal statutes when it issued the permits for the pipeline (Gilio-Whitaker, 2019: 3). This initially led to a re-routing of the pipeline away from the Missouri River. Additionally, the Sioux nation also appealed to the Office of the High Commissioner for Human Rights and UN Special Rapporteurs on human rights, after which the Standing Rock case appeared in several UN reports and statements (Tysiachniouk et al., 2021: 902).

Despite these initial legal victories, when Donald Trump was elected US President in 2016, he signed a new memorandum on the pipeline, throwing the support of the Executive branch of the US government behind the pipeline (Steinman, 2019: 1085). The Dakota Access Pipeline was finally completed in April 2017 and delivered oil the following month. The Sioux Tribe continued the legal fight, however, and two district judges in 2020 ordered the US Army Corps of Engineers to conduct a new environmental impact review which, as of 2022, is still ongoing.

As elaborated in the previous chapter, the US government's relation to Native American nations has historically been characterised by lawfare (often including actual warfare as well), competing jurisdictions, and grey legal areas leading to complex jurisprudence. This also goes for the persecution of Indigenous activists protesting land seizures through mobilisations. Arguing for a direct correlation between the mass incarceration of Natives and the violent suppression of political dissent, Estes notes that South Dakota's prison population increased 500% from the 1973 Wounded Knee/Standing Rock protests to 2012, with 30% of the prison population being Native although they make up only 9% of the total population (2017: 118). Similarly, there is a long history of tribal groups fighting legal battles against the US government to secure environmental justice, tribal sovereignty and rights, as well as environmental, cultural, or religious self-determination (Johnson, 2017: 155).

As Crepelle notes, although the Sioux have a well-documented history of resisting the US government and fighting injustices against their land and people, the contemporary 'battle' for Standing Rock is not military, but is rather fought in federal courtrooms (2018: 142). The Sioux nation's status as a federally recognised tribe gives them the legal rights necessary to protect their land, water, and air and provides the very foundation for the practice of asymmetric lawfare. This stands in stark contrast to other Native nations without federal recognition who are legally powerless to stop exploitation from oil and gas companies. This federal recognition is most often achieved through legislation, meaning many Native nations already have experience in legal activism (ibid.: 149). Native nations have used their sovereign status to create particularised environmental standards on their lands.

The protests in North and South Dakota also show new avenues for Indigenous communities to protect traditional sacred sites and practices through new allies and alternative legal strategies, or what we term civil society or bottom-up lawfare. Steinman argues that the DAPL protests' initial success lay in the diverse tactics used by activists combining legal avenues with direct action, and in the alliance between Indigenous activists and non-Native environmentalists (2019: 1085). In her analysis of the protests, Gilio-Whitaker likewise notes that effective partnerships with allies in the environmental movement is the best path for Indigenous movements to secure environmental justice objectives for 'Native and non-Native alike' (2019: 162).

Critical voices such as Estes argue that when it comes to Federal Indian Law, 'the arc of the Western moral universe never bends towards Indigenous justice' (2019: 230). However, others have argued that Indigenous bottom-up lawfare has had a meaningful impact over the past decades, most notably in the Native American Graves Protection and Repatriation Act (US Congress, 1990). Gilio-Whitaker argues that Indigenous peoples rarely experience Western law as fair, but rather as an enforcer of oppression (2019: 36). This is precisely why the civil society lawfare of the DAPL protests is important, as it showcases the power Indigenous activists can have when they are able to use the law to protect their rights and combat adversaries with superior resources using asymmetric lawfare.

5.4 Lawfare from 'weak' governmental actors

Lawfare from below is not only conducted by civil society groups but may also be carried out by other weak actors. This includes small states or sub-state governments punching above their weight and using international law instruments to challenge a stronger adversary, a task which would not be possible through conventional military means. However, for weak actors, the use of asymmetric lawfare suffers from the same structural constraints as any other strategic action path in the face of a stronger adversary, namely limited chance of success due to power imbalance. In Chapter 2, we analysed the doctrines and applications of lawfare by great powers in the geopolitical sphere. Inverting the telescope, this section focuses on the use of lawfare by less powerful actors, including weak states and sub-state polities.

One of these sub-state actors is Catalonia. In this case, which we thoroughly analysed in the previous chapter, policymakers from the autonomous government have engaged in asymmetric counter-lawfare in response to Spanish central government state lawfare. This has primarily involved substantial attempts to internationalise and *Europeanise* the conflict through foreign and supranational courts, in some cases generating bilateral problems between Spain and fellow EU member states harbouring Catalan politicians in exile. In a significant Catalan legal victory, the Brussels Court of Appeals refused to extradite Lluís Puig, a former Catalan government minister living in exile in Brussels, contending that his fundamental legal rights could be at risk if extradited as 'the right to a fair trial is not guaranteed in Spain' (Hope, 2021). Similar defeats for the Spanish judiciary have taken place in other European courts where the Spanish judiciary successively failed to extradite pro-secession policymakers. Former Catalan President Carles Puigdemont has notoriously avoided separate cases of extradition from Belgian, German, and Italian courts since going into exile in November 2017, gaining significant legal victories over Spain in the process.

Further, exiled Catalan policymakers have made numerous attempts at appealing court decisions throughout the Spanish legal system, despite their explicit lack of trust in the Spanish legal system with little if any prospect of success appealing to Spanish courts (Catalan News, 2021). This is explained by the fact that to bring a case before the European Court of Human Rights (ECHR), the case must have been appealed in all national courts. In this court, actors 'seek justice', through asymmetric lawfare in the form of compensation for former prisoners and exiled policymakers in supranational courts which are perceived as more neutral than their Spanish counterparts, and further their internationalisation of the Catalan conflict.[9] Several cases have already been brought to the ECHR, but as of April 2022, all cases have been rejected.

While very few studies have focused on lawfare and counter-lawfare in the context of the Catalan dispute (cf. Antentas, 2021), the literature is abound with examples of different forms of lawfare in the Israeli-Palestinian conflict (Weizman, 2010; Dunlap, 2015; Kittrie, 2016; Trachtman, 2016). Kittrie goes so far as to label the Palestine–Israeli conflict a 'lawfare laboratory' (2016: 197). This section will focus on the use of Palestinian asymmetrical lawfare to challenge Israel. In recent years, the Palestinian lawfare strategy has experienced some success. For instance, with the support of various UN member states, the Palestinian government managed to request an advisory opinion from the International Court of Justice (ICJ) in 2003 regarding the legality of the Israeli West Bank wall. The ICJ's opinion, which explicitly concluded that the construction of said wall was 'contrary to international law' (ICJ, 2004: 12), represented a clear triumph for the Palestinian strategy of asymmetric lawfare.

A fundamental pillar of the Palestinian lawfare strategy is deterring Israeli warfare operations through the threat of international prosecution for perpetrators of alleged war crimes. This strategy was considerably strengthened in April 2015, when Palestine joined the ICC. According to Clancy and Falk, such membership served two purposes, namely to seek justice for victims of Israeli military actions and to advance the liberation struggle (2021). In the same vein, Palestinian Prime Minister Mohammad Shtayyeh explicitly stated that ICC membership was a useful instrument for furthering Palestine's interests and to 'internationalise the conflict' (cited by Browning, 2015).

In short, Palestinian membership of the ICC opens the door to indicting Israeli soldiers[10] in The Hague. This possibility, albeit still remote, gained traction in February 2021, when the Pre-Trial Chamber of the ICC confirmed its jurisdiction over Palestine (International Criminal Court, 2021). Despite the potentiality of Palestine's lawfare victories, it remains unclear how this success will translate into concrete legal and political victories such as the actual prosecution of Israeli security forces or the international legal recognition of Palestinian statehood. Such limitations are a constant in asymmetric lawfare, which is often undertaken as a last resort.

The *Nicaragua v. United States* case in the ICJ, examined in Chapter 2, provides a clear illustration of the inherent shortcomings of asymmetric lawfare. While the Central American nation managed to achieve an astounding legal victory when the court deemed Washington's policies, such as laying mines in civilian harbours and supporting terrorist groups, as unlawful (ICJ, 1986), this did not have any significant legal effect. On the contrary, the US disregarded the court ruling by continuing with its foreign policies in Central America and by refusing to pay a single dollar in compensation to Nicaragua. Displaying a blatant disregard for the court and international law in general, the US State Department unilaterally concluded that the ICJ was 'not equipped to deal with a case of this nature' (cited by Jenkins, 1986). The US' downright dismissal of the ICJ's final decision has been termed as an 'abject failure of the law' (Fichtelberg, 2016: 165). While highly illustrative, this case is not the only one demonstrating the difficulties of asymmetrical lawfare and the hostility of great powers towards international law when it challenges their foreign policy.

Another example from Chapter 2, the *Philippines v. China* case at the Permanent Court of Arbitration (PCA), offers additional evidence of the fragilities of lawfare conducted by weak actors. In 2013, the Republic of the Philippines brought an arbitration against the People's Republic of China (PRC) at the PCA to counter Chinese sovereignty claims over maritime areas in the South China Sea such as the Spratly Islands (Philippine's Foreign Ministry, 2013). The court unequivocally supported the Philippines's claim, ruling that 'there was no legal basis for China to claim historic rights' (Permanent Court of Arbitration, 2016: 2) and that China's construction of artificial islands for military purposes was unlawful (ibid.: 4). The PRC followed the 4-NOs formula ('No Acceptance, No Participation, No Recognition and No Implementation'), declaring the ruling as void, null, and 'not binding' for China (Chinese Ministry of Foreign Affairs, 2016).

One of the clearest illustrations of the powerlessness of the PCA decision is that China steadfastly continued building its military capabilities in the Spratly Islands after it, regardless. The same year of the ruling, the Philippines Foreign Minister acknowledged that Manila was helpless vis-à-vis the Chinese military might: '[W]e cannot stop China . . . there is nothing that we can do about it' (cited by Reuters, 2016). Similarly, the President of the Philippines, Rodrigo Duterte, confirmed the uselessness of the ruling when, in 2021, pointed out that 'in real life between nations that paper [the PCA ruling] is nothing' (cited by CNN Philippines, 2021). It is, therefore, not too far-fetched to argue that the legal victory in the PCA was more symbolic than real for the Philippines.

More recently, in March 2022, Ukraine instituted proceedings against Russia in the ICJ with the objective of halting the latter's invasion (International Court of Justice, 2022b). The court accepted Ukraine's request and urged Russia to provisionally 'suspend the military operations that it commenced on 24 February 2022' (ibid.: 17). At the time of this writing, in April 2022, the ICJ's provisional order has had no effect whatsoever regarding Russia's 'special operation' in Ukraine, despite being legally binding. As seen in previous paragraphs, it would not be the first time that a great power disregards legally binding decisions from legal supranational institutions.

5.5 Conclusion

This chapter has explored asymmetric lawfare, an instrument increasingly used by civil society actors, particularly groups that focus on environmental and human rights issues. This use can be explained by the fact that, when coupled with more traditional forms of mobilised activism such as protests, civil disobedience, and media campaigns, asymmetric lawfare can be a potent weapon in the fight for social justice. We have illustrated the use of lawfare with two examples: the Ogoni case and the Dakota Access Pipeline protests.

One of the main challenges faced by asymmetric lawfare is the difficulty in venues that enable universal jurisdiction. This is particularly the case for civil society organisations seeking leverage over transnational companies or national governments. Fundamentally, non-state actors lack institutions where they can bring their cases to. This chapter has shown that the ATS bill in the US seemingly offered a chance to address cases of human rights abuses (regardless of where they were committed), but the 2013 Supreme Court ruling *Kiobel v. Royal Dutch Petroleum Co.* clearly closed the door to that possibility (2013). For their part, while weak states have direct access to international courts such as the ICJ and the ICC, their prospects of success are extremely limited. This is palpable even in cases in which these actors manage to achieve initial lawfare victories, such as Nicaragua's contentious case in the ICJ in the mid-1980s. This case illustrates that while 'weak' actors may achieve some gains via asymmetric lawfare in international courts, great powers maintain the power necessary to blatantly ignore adversary rulings condemning their actions. In simple terms, they can get away with violating international law. Likewise, for sub-state governments attempting to level the playing field vis-à-vis central governments, the stronger, established state actors often have the power to ignore international court rulings in favour of the weaker party.

In conclusion, asymmetrical lawfare, whether conducted by civil society or by weak governmental actors, is characterised by a common negative feature: significant limitations in actual gains. As the Comaroffs argue, while the weak may resort to lawfare, they do not 'predominate' (2006: 31) in this domain for the very inescapable tautology that they lack power, and litigation privileges the powerful (ibid., 2009). While the use of asymmetric lawfare may provide some leverage and even symbolic victories for 'weak' actors, the structural hierarchies inherent to political conflict tend to favour the stronger parties in the end. Since asymmetric lawfare has poor prospects of success, it is attractive primarily as a form of drawn-out legal attrition, a supportive element of a larger political strategy, or as a last-ditch attempt to resist much stronger adversaries.

Notes

1 Particularly in the US, Winkler illustrates how corporations have fought for their supposed constitutional rights, most notably the right to 'spend money to influence elections', or lobbying (2018: 6).
2 According to Setzer and Higham, the courts have ruled in favour of climate change advocates in 58% of the concluded cases (outside the US) dealing with climate change issues (2021: 19).
3 For further details on the ICC, see Chapter 2.
4 Despite the fact that the case is considered a 'model' for universal jurisdiction, Judge Garzón failed to extradite Pinochet from London.
5 They had been found guilty by a military appointed tribunal of 'incitement to murder' of four Ogoni elders who opposed MOSOP (Boele *et al.*, 2001).
6 The CCR filed three lawsuits: *Wiwa v. Royal Dutch Petroleum*, *Wiwa v. Anderson*, and *Wiwa v. Shell Petroleum Development Company*.
7 According to the ATS, '[T]he district courts shall have original jurisdiction of any civil action by an alien for a tort only, committed in violation of the law of nations or a treaty of the United States' (quoted by Congressional Research Service, 2022: 1). The ATS was only invoked three times between 1789 and 1956 (US Supreme Court, 2013).
8 Also known as the #NoDAPL movement.
9 These legal battles have even extended beyond territorial issues to policy areas such as climate change and environmental protection in lawfare struggles over minority 'green nationalism' (Conversi and Hau, 2021; Hau, 2022).
10 In December 2019, Fatou Bensouda, an ICC prosecutor, found that there was 'a reasonable basis to believe that' members of the Israeli security forces had committed war crimes during the 2014 Gaza conflict (International Criminal Court, 2020: 1).

Chapter 6

Conclusion

One of the central arguments of this book has been that lawfare is a polysemantic concept used by a wide range of actors to accomplish political objectives. As such, we view lawfare as a concept with multiple dimensions. In our conceptualisation, we outline these dimensions as geopolitical lawfare, domestic lawfare, state lawfare, and asymmetric lawfare. This segmentation into multiple types allows us to broaden our understanding of lawfare, incorporating its various contours and analytical applications. Our typological division is based on three key factors:

a) **Who** applies lawfare (governmental or civil society actor)
b) In which **context** (domestic or international)
c) And what **political objective** lies behind it (power accumulation, undermining opposition, defending human rights, protecting the territorial status quo)

The common element present in all the dimensions of lawfare we explore in this book is the instrumentalisation of legal means to pursue political objectives. We find it important to note that strategies of lawfare are by no means restricted to 'evil', autocratic regimes or nefarious actors. One of the key findings of our book is that in principle, any actor – regardless of motive and power capabilities – can resort to lawfare. However, not all actors are equally successful in their use of lawfare, as it is a practice that is deeply context-dependent and relies on already existing power structures. With few exceptions, such as the Huawei example between the US and China examined in Chapter 2, there is an inherent power asymmetry involved in lawfare. Through numerous examples in this book, we have shown that weak actors are inherently less effective at securing political objectives through lawfare.

DOI: 10.4324/9781003289869-6

For instance, our analysis of geopolitical lawfare has demonstrated that since the international system is characterised by the lack of a superior authority with the capacity to enforce rulings, no legal supranational institution can currently coerce great powers to abide by international law.

One of the effects of this is that weak actors have an inherent and inescapable disadvantage. This creates the paradox that even when weaker political actors do manage to obtain legal victories in supranational courts such as the ICJ, these triumphs will likely be more symbolic than legally binding. As we argued in Chapter 2 and 5, more often than not great powers get away with international law infringements because of the structural logic of power politics, which tends to protect and empower the already powerful. For example, while both Nicaragua and the Philippines achieved remarkable legal victories at the ICJ (1986) and the PCA (2016), the respective great powers were able to largely ignore and dismiss these rulings.

Similarly, in Chapter 5 we show that asymmetric lawfare is often rather ineffective even when legally successful, and while it may be a valuable tool for social activists, it is certainly not a potent game-changer in conflicts that are already characterised by deep inequality. Consequently, geopolitical lawfare in the international arena appears to require a position of power in order to be truly effective and respects existing relations of power to an extent. In sum, a powerful actor using lawfare is more likely to succeed and benefit from the strategy than a disempowered actor engaging in asymmetric or counter-lawfare. As such, lawfare, whatever its dimension, is a political strategy that is fundamentally dependent on structural contexts of power, resources, and capacity.

This element of power asymmetry is also present in domestic lawfare and state lawfare, albeit in a different form. In these cases, the existence of a superior authority with coercive power directly plays against the interests of weak actors. Our argument that domestic lawfare constitutes *the most pernicious dimension of lawfare* goes in this direction. This dimension of lawfare implies a systematic effort 'to exert control over and/or to coerce political subjects by recourse to the violence inherent in legal instruments' (Comaroff and Comaroff, 2006: 49). Simply put, in domestic lawfare, hegemonic actors have the ability to consolidate their power by undermining – and neutralising – opponents through the judiciary.

This weaponisation of law is, of course, not cost-free as it could compromise the most fundamental pillars of liberal democracy, leading to democratic backsliding (see Bermeo, 2016). In Chapter 3, we distinguished between soft applications of lawfare, in the shape of executives accumulating power by undermining the independence of the judiciary, from more *active* forms of domestic lawfare in contexts where the judiciary is already deeply compromised. In the latter case, domestic lawfare can dramatically influence political processes. It can for instance, prevent candidates from contesting elections, send them to exile and even, like in the case of former Brazilian president Lula, lead to the incarceration of leading political figures.

In Chapter 4 we show that despite significant costs to democratic quality, state lawfare can be brutally effective when used by states to address territorial or secession conflicts. While territorial conflicts and secessionist disputes are inherently political phenomena, state lawfare involves moving disputes from the political to the judicial sphere. In that terrain, the central state clearly has the upper hand, being able to *legally define* the territorial order. This appears particularly clear in the case of the territorial dispossession of Native Americans, which was enacted primarily by legal means.

This inherent power asymmetry coupled with the alignment of judicial and executive interests does not provide incentives to political compromise. State lawfare can generate minority grievances and create fertile ground for conflict aggravation, as we saw with the Northern Irish case. In a process reminiscent of securitisation (Wæver, 1993), state lawfare emerges not only as a policy tool but a rhetorical framing device that shifts political conflicts to issues of national security, where the government can enact states of exception and temporarily halt fundamental civil liberties. Using legal tools to criminalise and delegitimise political struggle, state lawfare practices go beyond punishing only those individuals engaging in actual political violence, extending for example to the criminalisation of civil society groups with territorial agendas. Through legal states of exception and a rhetoric of war, governments using state lawfare turn citizens into enemy combatants without fundamental liberal rights. In this way, although effective in suppressing territorial conflicts in the short term, state lawfare may hamper long-term peaceful conflict resolution. Like domestic lawfare, it may also lead to the criminalisation of ideas and political movements.

Perhaps unsurprisingly, we foresee a bright future for the concept of lawfare: first, because of its attractiveness as a heuristic. The composite structure of lawfare combining 'law' and 'warfare' clearly conveys the idea of the weaponisation of legal instruments in conflictual dynamics. Second, as we have argued throughout the book, lawfare is flexible and elastic, and therefore can be applied to different contexts where actors use legal means instrumentally to pursue political aims. Third, the term is agent-centred, focusing on active processes of legal and political conflict. This makes it analytically valuable in a number of academic contexts such as studies of legal mobilisation, democratic backsliding, judicialisation, securitisation, great power competition, and internal territorial conflicts.

Last but not least, the growing presence of the phenomenon itself globally consolidates lawfare as a key concept that will continue influencing social, political, and academic debates. With this book, we hope to have opened debate on this multifaceted term as a new trajectory in law.

Bibliography

Agamben, Giorgio. *State of Exception*. University of Chicago Press, 2005.

Ali, Mohamed M., and Iqbal H. Shah. "Sanctions and childhood mortality in Iraq." *The Lancet* 355, no. 9218 (2000): 1851–1857.

Al Jazeera. "Libya Warns against UK Military Advisers," 2011. Available at: www. aljazeera.com/news/2011/4/20/libya-warns-against-uk-military-advisers

Allison, Roy. *Russia, the West, and Military Intervention*. Oxford University Press, 2013.

Alonso, Rogelio. "Why do terrorists stop? Analyzing why ETA members abandon or continue with terrorism." *Studies in Conflict & Terrorism* 34, no. 9 (2011): 696–716.

Altimira, Oriol Solé. "De detenida por terrorista a absuelta: los dos años de laberinto judicial de la CDR Tamara Carrasco." *ElDiario.es*, 2020. Available at: www. eldiario.es/catalunya/detenida-terrorista-absuelta-anos-laberinto-judicial-cdr-tamara-carrasco_1_6273052.html

Altimira, Oriol Solé. "La Fiscalía insiste en que la CDR Tamara Carrasco creó 'un entorno social violento' y recurre su absolución." *ElDiario.es*, 2021. Available at: www.eldiario.es/catalunya/fiscalia-insiste-cdr-tamara-carrasco-creo-entorno-social-violento-recurre-absolucion_1_8297708.html

Amnesty International. "Libertad de Expresión En España," 2022. Available at: www.es.amnesty.org/en-que-estamos/espana/libertad-de-expresion/

Amnesty International. "Spain: Macroproceso 18/98 trial highlights flaws in Spanish counter-terrorism legislation," 2009. Available at: www.amnesty.org/fr/wp-content/uploads/2021/07/eur410092009en.pdf

Amnesty International. "The power of the street. Protecting the right to peaceful protest in Poland," 2018. Available at: www.amnesty.org/en/documents/EUR37/8525/2018/en/

Anderson, Benedict. *Imagined Communities: Reflections on the Origin and Spread of Nationalism*. Verso, 1991.

Ansah, Tawia. "Lawfare: A rhetorical analysis." *Case Western Reserve Journal of International Law* 43 (2010): 87–119.

Antentas, Josep Maria. "Spain: The state, the regime crisis and the national question." *Socialism and Democracy* 35, no. 1 (2021): 51–78.

Arnold, Aaron. "The true costs of financial sanctions." *Survival* 58, no. 3 (2016): 77–100.

Arzoz, Xabier. "Constitutional court of Spain (Tribunal Constitucional de España)." In *Max Planck Encyclopedia of Comparative Constitutional Law*, edited by Rainer Grote, Frauke Lachenmann and Rüdiger Wolfrum, 639–703. Oxford University Press, 2018.

Asens, Jaume. "Presos políticos y sedición." *No hi ha dret* (blog), 2017. Available at: www.nohihadret.cat/2017/12/presos-politicos-y-sedicion/

Åtland, Kristian. "Redrawing borders, reshaping orders: Russia's quest for dominance in the Black Sea region." *European Security* 30, no. 2 (2021): 305–324.

Austin, W. Chadwick, and Antony Barone Kolenc. "Who's afraid of the big bad wolf? The international criminal court as a weapon of asymmetric warfare." *Vanderbilt Journal of Transnational Law* 39, no. 2 (2006): 291–292.

Averre, Derek, and Lance Davies. "Russia, humanitarian intervention and the responsibility to protect: The case of Syria." *International Affairs* 91, no. 4 (2015): 813–834.

Baer, George W. "Sanctions and security: The league of nations and the Italian–Ethiopian war, 1935–1936." *International Organization* 27, no. 2 (1973): 165–179.

Bale, Tim. "Will it all end in tears? What really happens when democracies use law to ban political parties." In *Regulating Political Parties. European Democracies in Comparative Perspective*, edited by Ingrid van Biezen and Hans-Martien ten Napel, 195–224. Leiden University Press, 2014.

Banta, Benjamin R. "Just war theory and the 2003 Iraq war forced displacement." *Journal of Refugee Studies* 21, no. 3 (2008): 261–284.

Barreiro, Belén, and Ignacio Sánchez-Cuenca. "In the whirlwind of the economic crisis: Local and regional elections in Spain, May 2011." *South European Society and Politics* 17, no. 2 (2012): 281–294.

Bartman, Christi Scott. "Lawfare and the definition of aggression: What the Soviet Union and Russian Federation can teach us." *Case Western Reserve Journal of International Law* 43 (2010): 423–445.

Basque Government. "Resultados electorales. Juntas Generales 2011", 2011. Available at: https://www.euskadi.eus/ab12aAREWar/resultado/maint#

Batista, Antoni. *Adiós a las armas: Una crónica del final de ETA*. Debate, 2012.

Bauomy, Jasmin. "Germany refuses to extradite Pole under European arrest warrant due to fair trial fears". *Euronews*, 2020. Available at: https://www.euronews.com/2020/03/09/germany-refuses-to-extradite-pole-under-european-arrest-warrant-due-to-fair-trial-fears

BBC. "Brazil's ex-President Lula convicted of corruption," 2017a. Available at: www.bbc.com/news/world-latin-america-40588992

BBC. "Catalonia: Did voters face worst police violence ever seen in the EU?," 2017b. Available at: www.bbc.com/news/world-europe-41677911

BBC. "Huawei finance chief Meng Wanzhou arrested in Canada," 2018. Available at: www.bbc.com/news/business-46462858

BBC. "Huawei's Meng Wanzhou flies back to China after deal with US," 2021a. Available at: www.bbc.com/news/world-us-canada-58682998

BBC. "Lula: Brazil ex-president's corruption convictions annulled," 2021b. Available at: www.bbc.com/news/world-latin-america-56326389

BBC. "NI Activates Internment Law," 1971. Available at: http://news.bbc.co.uk/onthisday/hi/dates/stories/august/9/newsid_4071000/4071849.stm

Bellamy, Alex. "Ethics and intervention: The 'humanitarian exception' and the problem of abuse in the case of Iraq." *Journal of Peace Research* 41, no. 2 (2004): 131–147.

Bermeo, Nancy. "On democratic backsliding." *Journal of Democracy* 27, no. 1 (2016): 5–19.

Black, Ian and Severin Carrell. "Russian arms shipment bound for Syria foiled by Britain's insurers." *The Guardian*, 2012. Available at: www.theguardian.com/world/2012/jun/19/syria-arms-shipment-foiled

BOE. "Law 54/1978," 1978b. Available at: www.boe.es/buscar/doc.php?id=BOE-A-1978-29843

BOE. "Organic law 10/1995," 1995. Available: www.boe.es/boe/dias/1995/11/24/

BOE. "Organic law 6/2002 on political parties," 2002. Available at: https://adsdatabase.ohchr.org/IssueLibrary/SPAIN_Organic%20Law%206-2002%20on%20political%20parties.pdf

BOE. "The Spanish Constitution," 1978a. Available at: www.boe.es/legislacion/documentos/ConstitucionINGLES.pdf

Boele, Richard, Heike Fabig and David Wheeler. "Shell, Nigeria and the Ogoni. A study in unsustainable development: I. The story of Shell, Nigeria and the Ogoni people – environment, economy, relationships: Conflict and prospects for resolution 1." *Sustainable Development* 9, no. 2 (2001): 74–86.

Bogaards, Matthijs. "De-democratization in Hungary: Diffusely defective democracy." *Democratization* 25, no. 8 (2018): 1481–1499.

Bogaards, Matthijs. "How to classify hybrid regimes? Defective democracy and electoral authoritarianism." *Democratization* 16, no. 2 (2009): 399–423.

Bossacoma, Pau. *Morality and Legality of Secession.* Springer, 2020.

Bourne, Angela. "Militant democracy and the banning of political parties in democratic states: Why some do and why some don't." In *Militant Democracy – Political Science, Law and Philosophy*, edited by Afshin Ellian and Bastiaan Rijpkema, 23–46. Springer International Publishing, 2018.

Bourne, Angela. "Why ban Batasuna? Terrorism, political parties and democracy." *Comparative European Politics* 13, no. 3 (2015): 325–344.

Boyle, Kevin, Tom Hadden, and Paddy Hillyard. *Law and State: The Case of Northern Ireland.* Law in Society Series. Robertson, 1975.

Bozóki, András, and Dániel Hegedűs. "An externally constrained hybrid regime: Hungary in the European Union." *Democratization* 25, no. 7 (2018): 1173–1189.

Branch, Adam. "Neither peace nor justice: Political violence and the peasantry in northern Uganda, 1986–1998." *African Studies Journal* 8, no. 2 (2005): 1–31.

Brännström, Leila. "Law, objectives of government, and regimes of truth: Foucault's understanding of law and the transformation of the law of the EU internal market." *Foucault Studies* 18 (2014): 173–194.

Brew, Joe. "The tall tale of violence." *VilaWeb*, 2018. Available at: https://english.vilaweb.cat/noticies/the-tall-tale-of-violence/

Browning, Noah. "Abbas trades stalemate for confrontation in ICC move." *Reuters*, 2015. Available at: www.reuters.com/article/us-palestinians-israel-abbas-idUSKBN0KA1NI20150101

Brown Swan, Coree, and Daniel Cetrà. "Why stay together? State nationalism and justifications for state unity in Spain and the UK." *Nationalism and Ethnic Politics* 26, no. 1 (2020): 46–65.

Burley, Anne-Marie. "The Alien Tort Statute and the Judiciary Act of 1789: A badge of honor." *American Journal of International Law* 83, no. 3 (1989): 461–493.

Burstein, Paul. "Legal mobilization as a social movement tactic: The struggle for equal employment opportunity." *American Journal of Sociology* 96, no. 5 (1991): 1201–1225.

Buzan, Barry, Ole Wæver, and Jaap De Wilde. *Security: A New Framework for Analysis*. Lynne Rienner Publishers, 1998.

Cai, Congyan. *The Rise of China and International Law: Taking Chinese Exceptionalism Seriously*. Oxford University Press, 2019.

Calderón Castillo, Javier. "El libreto del 'lawfare' contra Rafael Correa." *Celag*, 2018. Available at: www.celag.org/libreto-lawfare-contra-rafael-correa/

Carlson, John and Neville Yeomans. "Whither Goeth the law – humanity or barbarity." In *The Way Out – Radical Alternatives in Australia*, edited by Margareth Smith and David Crossley. Lansdowne Press, 1975. Available at: www.laceweb.org.au/whi.htm

Carr, Edward H. *The Twenty Years' Crisis: 1919–1939*. Palgrave Macmillan, 1939/2016.

Castan Pinos, Jaume. *Kosovo and the Collateral Effects of Humanitarian Intervention*. Routledge, 2019.

Castan Pinos, Jaume. "The challenge to territorial integrity: Kosovo and beyond." In *Diversity in Europe*, edited by Charlotte Gaitanides and Gerd Grözinger, 220–236. Nomos Verlag, 2015.

Castan Pinos, Jaume and Cathal McCall. "The division of Ireland and its foes: The centenary of resistance to partition." *Nations and Nationalism* 27, no. 3 (2021): 846–861.

Castan Pinos, Jaume and Jeremy Sacramento. "L'État contre-attaque: la contre-para-diplomatie espagnole face à la Catalogne (2012–2017)." *Relations Internationales* 179, no. 3 (2019): 95–111.

Castan Pinos, Jaume and Jeremy Sacramento. "The sovereignty paradox: Brexit's territorial consequences for Gibraltar, Scotland and Northern Ireland," DIIS Working Paper 2 (2020): 1–25.

Castan Pinos, Jaume and Steven M. Radil. "The territorial contours of terrorism: A conceptual model of territory for non-state violence." *Terrorism and Political Violence* 32, no. 5 (2020): 1027–1046.

Castellanos López, José Antonio. "Esquerra Republicana de Cataluña durante la transición democrática: el proceso hacia su legalización como partido político." *Historia Contemporánea* 28 (2016): 215–233.

Castellum.AI. "Russia Sanctions Dashboard," 2022. Available at: www.castellum.ai/russia-sanctions-dashboard

Catalan News. "Catalan independence v Spain: The legal battles at the European Court of Human Rights," 2021. Available at: www.catalannews.com/in-depth/item/catalan-independence-v-spain-the-legal-battles-at-the-european-court-of-human-rights

CBS News. "60 minutes," 1996. Available at: www.youtube.com/watch?v=FbIX1CP9qr4

CCR. "Kiobel v. Royal Dutch Petroleum Co.," 2018. Available at: https://ccrjustice.org/home/what-we-do/our-cases/kiobel-v-royal-dutch-petroleum-co-amicus

CCR. "Wiwa et al v. Royal Dutch Petroleum et al.," 2022. Available at: https://ccrjustice.org/home/what-we-do/our-cases/wiwa-et-al-v-royal-dutch-petroleum-et-al

Cheng, Dean. "Winning without fighting: Chinese legal warfare." *Backgrounder* 2692 (2012): 1–11.

Chifu, Iulian. "Lawfare: Fighting with the legal framework and reaching military objectives by using the law." In *The Changing Face of Warfare in the 21st Century*, edited by Greg Simons and Iulian Chifu, 80–117. Routledge, 2017.

China Daily. "Germany rejects US sanctions threat over Nord Stream 2 pipeline," 2020. Available at: www.chinadaily.com.cn/a/202007/17/WS5f10fedba31083481725a1a4.html

Chinese Ministry of Foreign Affairs. "China does not accept or recognize the South China Sea Arbitration by the Philippines," 2016. Available at: www.mfa.gov.cn/ce/cgzur//det/szyw/t1356937.htm

Chinese Ministry of Foreign Affairs. "Wang Yi laid out three basic facts of the issue of the South China Sea," 2020. Available at: www.mfa.gov.cn/ce/cgadelaide//eng/zgxw/t1814210.htm

Chomsky, Noam. "Humanitarian imperialism: The new doctrine of imperial right." *Monthly Review* 60, no. 4 (2008): 22–50.

Chomsky, Noam, and Michel Foucault. *The Chomsky-Foucault Debate: On Human Nature*. New Press, 2015.

Christensen, Thomas J. "Fostering stability or creating a monster? The rise of China and US policy toward East Asia." *International Security* 31, no. 1 (2006): 81–126.

Cianetti, Licia, James Dawson and Seán Hanley. "Rethinking 'Democratic Backsliding' in Central and Eastern Europe – looking beyond Hungary and Poland." *East European Politics* 34, no. 3 (2018): 243–256.

Ciocchini, Paolo, and Stéfanie Khoury. "The 'war on terror' and Spanish state violence against Basque political dissent." In *Counter-Terrorism and State Political Violence: The "war on Terror" as Terror*, edited by Scott Poynting and David Whyte, 178–196. Routledge, 2012.

Clancy, Pearce, and Richard Falk. "The ICC and Palestine: Breakthrough and end of the road?" *Journal of Palestine Studies* 50, no. 3 (2021): 56–68.

Clarín. "La conspirativa teoría de Cristina," 2021. Available at: www.clarin.com/politica/ministro-justicia-jefa-espias-organizan-conferencia-lawfare-america-latina_0_di2oDAlZn.html

Clark, Cristy P. "The politics of public interest environmental litigation: lawfare in Australia." *Australian Environment Review* 31, no. 7 (2016): 258–262.

Clausewitz, Carl von. *On War*. Princeton University Press, 1984.

CNN Philippines. "Duterte says PH arbitral win vs. China 'just' a piece of paper, trash to be thrown away," 2021. Available at: www.cnnphilippines.com/news/2021/5/6/Duterte-PH-arbitral-win-vs.-China-a-piece-of-paper.html

Cohn, Ellen B. "Torture in the international community – problems of definition and limitation – the case of Northern Ireland note." *Case Western Reserve Journal of International Law* 11, no. 1 (1979): 159–186.

Comaroff, Jean and John L. Comaroff. *Ethnicity, Inc.* University of Chicago Press, 2009.

Comaroff, Jean and John L. Comaroff. "Law and disorder in the postcolony: An introduction." In *Law and Disorder in the Postcolony*, edited by Jean Comaroff and John Comaroff, 1–56. University of Chicago Press, 2006.

Comaroff, Jean and John L. Comaroff. "Law and disorder in the postcolony." *Social Anthropology* 15, no. 2 (2007): 133–152.

Comaroff, Jean and John L. Comaroff. "Millennial capitalism: First thoughts on a second coming." In *Millennial Capitalism and the Culture of Neoliberalism*, edited by Jean Comaroff and John Comaroff, 1–56. Duke University Press, 2001.

Comaroff, John L. "Colonialism, culture, and the law: A foreword." *Law & Social Inquiry* 26, no. 2 (2001): 305–314.

Congressional Research Service. "The Alien Tort Statute: A primer," 2022. Available at: https://sgp.fas.org/crs/misc/R44947.pdf

Constitution of the Republic of Uzbekistan. "Article 74", 2003. Available at: https://www.un.int/uzbekistan/uzbekistan/constitution-republic-uzbekistan

Conversi, Daniele, and Mark F. Hau. "Green nationalism. Climate action and environmentalism in left nationalist parties." *Environmental Politics* 30, no. 7 (2021): 1089–1110. https://doi.org/10.1080/09644016.2021.1907096

Coogan, Tim. *The Troubles: Ireland's Ordeal and the Search for Peace*. Palgrave Macmillan, 2002.

Correa, Rafael. "El lawfare en Ecuador." *Youtube*, 2021. Available at: www.youtube.com/watch?v=5tThrlKo8P4&t=2036s

Corrigan, Patrick. *Paper Trail: From Northern Ireland's Hooded Men to CIA's Global Torture*. Amnesty International, 2014. Available at: www.amnesty.org.uk/blogs/belfast-and-beyond/paper-trail-northern-ireland%E2%80%99s-hooded-men-cia%E2%80%99s-global-torture

Cram, Ian. "Constitutional responses to extremist political associations – ETA, Batasuna and democratic norms." *Legal Studies* 28, no. 1 (2008): 68–95.

Crepelle, Adam. "Standing Rock in the swamp: Oil, the environment, and the United Houma Nation's struggle for federal recognition." *Loyola Law Review* 64, no. 1 (2018): 141–186.

Cué, Carlos E. "Spanish PM announces legal changes to make banks pay mortgage tax." *El País*, 2018. Available at: https://english.elpais.com/elpais/2018/11/07/inenglish/1541605630_176759.html

Dardanelli, Paolo, and James Mitchell. "An independent Scotland? The Scottish National Party's bid for independence and its prospects." *The International Spectator* 49, no. 3 (2014): 88–105.

Davis, Lance, and Stanley Engerman. "History lessons: Sanctions-neither war nor peace." *Journal of Economic Perspectives* 17, no. 2 (2003): 187–197.

Deutsche Welle. "Ecuador's Rafael Correa requests asylum in Belgium: report," 2018. Available at: www.dw.com/en/ecuadors-rafael-correa-requests-asylum-in-belgium-report/a-46217705

Dewar, Michael. *The British Army in Northern Ireland.* Arms & Armour, 1996.

Diamond, Larry. *In Search of Democracy.* Routledge, 2016.

Dickson, Brice. "The detention of suspected terrorists in Northern Ireland and Great Britain." *University of Richmond Law Review* 43, no. 3 (2009): 927–966.

Dixon, Paul. *Northern Ireland: The Politics of War and Peace.* Palgrave Macmillan, 2008.

Drake, Charles JM. "The role of ideology in terrorists' target selection." *Terrorism and Political Violence* 10, no. 2 (1998): 53–85.

Drezner, Daniel W. "Targeted sanctions in a world of global finance." *International Interactions* 41, no. 4 (2015): 755–764.

Drezner, Daniel W. *The Sanctions Paradox: Economic Statecraft and International Relations.* Cambridge University Press, 1999.

Drezner, Daniel W. "The United States of sanctions: The use and abuse of economic coercion," *Foreign Affairs* 2021, no. 5 (2021): 142–154.

Drinoczi, Timea and Agnieszka Bień-Kacała. "Illiberal constitutionalism: The case of Hungary and Poland." *German Law Journal* 20, no. 8 (2019): 1140–1166.

Dunlap, Charles J. "Does lawfare need an apologia?," *Case Western Reserve Journal of International Law* 43, no. 2 (2010): 121–143.

Dunlap, Charles J. "Law and military interventions: Preserving humanitarian values in 21st conflicts." *Carr Center for Human Rights Policy*, 2001. Available at: https://people.duke.edu/~pfeaver/dunlap.pdf

Dunlap, Charles J. "Lawfare 101: A primer." *Military Review* 97, no. 3 (2017): 8–17.

Dunlap, Charles J. "Lawfare amid warfare." *Washington Times*, 2007. Available at: www.washingtontimes.com/news/2007/aug/03/lawfare-amidwarfare

Dunlap, Charles J. "Lawfare today: A perspective." *Yale Journal of International Affairs* 3, no. 1 (2008): 146–154.

Dunlap, Charles J. "Lawfare: A decisive element of 21st-century conflicts?," *Joint Force Quarterly* 54, no. 3 (2009): 34–39.

Dunlap, Charles J. "Lawfare." In *National Security Law*, edited by John Norton Moore, Guy Roberts and Robert F. Turner, 823–838. Carolina Academic Press, 2015.

Dworkin, Ronald M. "What is the rule of law?," *The Antioch Review* 30, no. 2 (1970): 151–155.

ECHR. "Ireland v. United Kingdom – 5310/71," 1978. Available at: www.worldlii.org/eu/cases/ECHR/1978/1.html

ECHR. "Del Río Prada v. Spain - 42750/09," 2013. Available at: https://hudoc.echr.coe.int/eng?i=001-127697#{%22itemid%22:[%22001-127697%22]}

EIU. "Democracy Index 2021: the China challenge." *The Economist*, 2022. Available at: https://pages.eiu.com/rs/753-RIQ-438/images/eiu-democracy-index-2021.pdf

Eskander, Shaikh, Sam Fankhauser and Joana Setzer. "Global lessons from climate change legislation and litigation." *Environmental and Energy Policy and the Economy* 2, no. 1 (2021): 44–82.

Estes, Nick. "Fighting for our lives: #NoDAPL in historical context." *Wicazo Sa Review* 32, no. 2 (2017): 115–122.

Estes, Nick. *Our History Is the Future: Standing Rock Versus the Dakota Access Pipeline, and the Long Tradition of Indigenous Resistance.* Verso Books, 2019.

ETA. "16 April 2018 Communiqué," 2018. Available at: www.eldiario.es/euskadi/documento-carta-eta-anuncia-disolucion_1_2142705.html

ETA. "20 October 2011 Communiqué," 2011. Available at: www.theguardian.com/world/2011/oct/20/basque-ceasefire-statement-full-text

ETA. "Principios," 1962. Available at: the Lazkao Benedictine Monastery Archive.

Europa Press. "Interpol rechaza por tercera vez emitir su 'alerta roja' contra el expresidente ecuatoriano Rafael Correa," 2021. Available at: www.europapress.es/internacional/noticia-interpol-rechaza-tercera-vez-emitir-alerta-roja-contra-expresidente-ecuatoriano-rafael-correa-20210818233148.html

European Commission. "Proposal for a Council decision on the determination of a clear risk of a serious breach by the Republic of Poland of the rule of law," 2017. Available at: https://eur-lex.europa.eu/legal-content/EN/TXT/PDF/?uri=CELEX:52017PC0835&from=EN

European Commission. "The 2019 EU justice scoreboard," 2019. Available at: http://dx.publications.europa.eu/10.2838/569

Falk, Richard. "Positive and negative forms of 'Lawfare'." *Foreign Policy Journal* (2015). Available at: www.foreignpolicyjournal.com/2015/02/24/positive-and-negative-forms-of-lawfare/

Falkner, Robert. "The Paris Agreement and the new logic of international climate politics." *International Affairs* 92, no. 5 (2016): 1107–1125.

Farrell, Michael. *Northern Ireland: The Orange State.* Pluto Press, 1976.

Fay, Derick. "Neoliberal conservation and the potential for lawfare: New legal entities and the political ecology of litigation at Dwesa–Cwebe, South Africa." *Geoforum* 44 (2013): 170–181.

Ferejohn, John. "Judicializing politics, politicizing law." *Law and Contemporary Problems* 65, no. 3 (2002): 41.

Fichtelberg, Aaron. *Law at the Vanishing Point: A Philosophical Analysis of International Law.* Routledge, 2016.

Finucane, Brian. "Time for the Biden administration to disavow the dangerous Soleimani legal opinions." *Just Security*, 2022. Available at: www.justsecurity.org/79700/time-for-the-biden-administration-to-disavow-the-dangerous-soleimani-legal-opinions/

Fisher, Kirsten J., and Cristina G. Stefan. "The ethics of international criminal 'Lawfare'." *International Criminal Law Review* 16, no. 2 (2016): 237–257.

Fletcher, Matthew. "A short history of Indian Law in the Supreme Court." *American Bar Association*, 2014. Available at: www.americanbar.org/groups/crsj/publications/human_rights_magazine_home/2014_vol_40/vol – 40 – no – 1 – tribal-sovereignty/short_history_of_indian_law/

Foucault, Michel. *Discipline and Punish: The Birth of the Prison.* Penguin, 2019a.

Foucault, Michel. *Power: The Essential Works of Michel Foucault 1954–1984*. Penguin, 2019b.

Foucault, Michel. *"Society Must Be Defended": Lectures at the Collège de France, 1975–1976*. Picador, 2003.

France 24. "Russia seizes three Ukrainian ships in Black Sea after firing on them," 2018. Available at: www.france24.com/en/20181125-ukraine-russia-seizes-three-ships-black-sea-crimea-fsb-navy

Franck, Thomas M. "Lessons of Kosovo." *American Journal of International Law* 93, no. 4 (1999): 857–860.

Freedom House. "Hungary: Freedom in the World 2022 country report," 2022. Available at: https://freedomhouse.org/country/hungary/freedom-world/2022

Gagnon, Alain-G. "Majority, state nationalism, and new research pathways." *Nationalism and Ethnic Politics* 26, no. 1 (2020): 85–93.

Giddens, Anthony. *The Constitution of Society: Outline of the Theory of Structuration*. Polity Press, 1984.

Gilio-Whitaker, Dina. *As Long as Grass Grows: The Indigenous Fight for Environmental Justice, from Colonization to Standing Rock*. Beacon Press, 2019.

GlobalFirePower. "2021 Military Strength Ranking," 2022. Available at: www.globalfirepower.com/countries-listing.php

Gloppen, Siri. "Conceptualizing lawfare: A typology & theoretical framework." *Center of Law and Social Transformation Paper*, (2018): 1–31.

Gloppen, Siri, and Asuncion Lera St Clair. "Climate change lawfare." *Social Research: An International Quarterly* 79, no. 4 (2012): 899–930.

Gobierno Argentino. "El Lawfare en América Latina y su impacto en la vigencia de los derechos humanos," 2021. Available at: www.argentina.gob.ar/sites/default/files/programa_final_web.pdf

Goetting, Nathan. "The Marshall Trilogy and the constitutional dehumanization of American Indians." *Guild Practitioner* 65 (2008): 207–226.

Goldenziel, Jill I. "Law as a battlefield: The US, China, and global escalation of lawfare." *Cornell Law Review* 106 (2020): 1085–1172.

Goldsmith, Jack. "The self-defeating International Criminal Court." *The University of Chicago Law Review* 70, no. 1 (2003): 89–104.

Goldstein, Judith L., Miles Kahler, Robert O. Keohane and Anne-Marie Slaughter. *Legalization and World Politics*. MIT Press, 2001.

Google Books Ngram Viewer "Lawfare, Judicialisation, abusive constitutionalism," 2022. Available at: https://books.google.com/ngrams

Gordon, Neve. "Human rights as a security threat: Lawfare and the campaign against human rights NGOs." *Law & Society Review* 48, no. 2 (2014): 311–344.

Gowlland-Debbas, Vera. *United Nations Sanctions and International Law*. Brill, 2021.

Greenwald, Glenn and Victor Pougy. "Hidden plot." *The Intercept*, 2019. Available at: https://theintercept.com/2019/06/09/brazil-car-wash-prosecutors-workers-party-lula/

Greenwood, Christopher. *International Law Reports*. Cambridge University Press, 1980.

Guardiola-Rivera, Oscar. "Memoirs of the plague: Lawfare." *Law and Critique* 32, no. 2 (2021): 139–146.

Guelke, Adrian. "The political impasse in South Africa and Northern Ireland: A comparative perspective." *Comparative Politics* 23, no. 2 (1991): 143–162.

Guilfoyle, Douglas. "The rule of law and maritime security: Understanding lawfare in the South China Sea." *International Affairs* 95, no. 5 (2019): 999–1017.

Halmai, Gábor. "Populism, authoritarianism and constitutionalism." *German Law Journal* 20, no. 3 (2019): 296–313.

Hamill, Desmond. *Pig in the Middle: The Army in Northern Ireland, 1969–1985.* Methuen, 1986.

Hamlin, Rebecca, and Gemma Sala. "The judicialization of politics disentangled." In *Oxford Research Encyclopedia of Politics.* Oxford University Press, 2018.

Handmaker, Jeff. "Lawfare against academics and the potential of legal mobilization as counterpower." In *Enforcing Silence: Academic Freedom, Palestine and the Criticism of Israel*, edited by David Landy, Ronit Lentin and Conor McCarthy, 233–260. Zed, 2020.

Handmaker, Jeff. Researching legal mobilisation and lawfare. Working Paper no. 641 (2019): 1–19.

Haque, Adil. "The Trump administration's latest (failed) attempt to justify the Soleimani strike." *Just Security*, 2020. Available at: www.justsecurity.org/69163/the-trump-administrations-latest-failed-attempt-to-justify-the-soleimani-strike/

Hau, Mark F. "From local concerns to global challenges: Continuity and change in sub-state 'green nationalism.'" *Frontiers in Political Science* 3 (2022): 1–13.

Hau, Mark F. *Negotiating Nationalism: National Identity, Party Ideology, and Ideas of Europe in the Scottish National Party and Esquerra Republicana de Catalunya* (PhD Thesis). Aarhus University, 2019.

Hayes, Mark. "The imposition of internment without trial in Northern Ireland, August 1971: Causes, consequences and lessons." In *The Politics of Criminology: Critical Studies on Deviance and Social Control*, edited by Stratos Georgoulas, 117–132. LIT Verlag, 2012.

Hayes, Patrick, and Jim Campbell. *Bloody Sunday: Trauma, Pain and Politics.* Pluto Press, 2005.

Hennessey, Thomas. *The Northern Ireland Peace Process: Ending the Troubles?* Gill & Macmillan, 1999.

Hennessy, Mark. "British Ministers sanctioned torture of NI internees." *The Irish Times*, 2021. Available at: www.irishtimes.com/news/politics/british-ministers-sanctioned-torture-of-ni-internees-1.1820882

Hidalgo Andrade, Gabriel. "La ficción del Lawfare." *PlanV*, 2018. Available at: www.planv.com.ec/ideas/ideas/la-ficcion-del-lawfare

Hirschl, Ran. "The judicialization of mega-politics and the rise of political courts." *Annual Review of Political Science* 11, no. 1 (2008): 93–118.

Hirschl, Ran. "The judicialization of politics." In *The Oxford Handbook of Political Science*, edited by Robert E. Goodin, 253–274. Oxford University Press, 2011.

Holmes, Stephen. "Lineages of the rule of law." In *Democracy and the Rule of Law*, edited by Adam Przeworski and José María Maravall, 19–61. Cambridge University Press, 2003.

Hong, Nong. *UNCLOS and Ocean Dispute Settlement: Law and Politics in the South China Sea.* Routledge, 2012.

Hope, Alan. "Brussels court rejects extradition of Catalan politician to Spain." *The Brussels Times*, 2021. Available at: www.brusselstimes.com/148639/brussels-court-rejects-extradition-of-catalan-politician-to-spain

House of Commons. "Reports of the Bloody Sunday inquiry," 2010. Available at: https://assets.publishing.service.gov.uk/government/uploads/system/uploads/attachment_data/file/279133/0029_i.pdf

Human Rights Council. "Information note on Human Rights Committee," 2018. Available at: www.ohchr.org/en/press-releases/2018/08/information-note-human-rights-committee?LangID=E&NewsID=23464

Human Rights Council. "Opinions adopted by the Working Group on Arbitrary Detention at its eighty-fourth session," 2019. Available at: https://documents-dds-ny.un.org/doc/UNDOC/GEN/G19/158/75/PDF/G1915875.pdf?OpenElement

Human Rights Council. "Visit to Spain – Report of the Special Rapporteur on minority issues," 2020. Available at: www.ohchr.org/EN/HRBodies/HRC/RegularSessions/Session43/Documents/A_HRC_43_47_Add.1_AdvanceEditedVersion.docx

Humlebæk, Carsten, and Mark F. Hau. "From national holiday to independence day: Changing perceptions of the 'Diada.'" *Genealogy* 4, no. 1 (2020): 125–148.

Hunt, Alan, and Gary Wickham. *Foucault and Law: Towards a Sociology of Law as Governance*. Pluto Press, 1994.

Hunt, Stacie. "The judicialization of politics in Canada and the United States." *Honors Projects* 39 (2013): 23.

Hurd, Ian. "Is humanitarian intervention legal? The rule of law in an incoherent world." *Ethics & International Affairs* 25, no. 3 (2011): 293–313.

Independent International Commission on Kosovo. *The Kosovo Report; Conflict, International Response, Lessons Learned*. Oxford University Press, 2000.

International Court of Justice. "Accordance with International Law of the Unilateral Declaration of Independence in Respect of Kosovo, Advisory Opinion," 2010. Available at: www.icj-cij.org/public/files/case-related/141/141-20100722-ADV-01-00-EN.pdf

International Court of Justice. "Case concerning Maritime Dispute (Peru v. Chile)," 2014. Available at: www.icj-cij.org/public/files/case-related/137/137-20140127-JUD-01-00-EN.pdf

International Court of Justice. "How the court works," 2022a. Available at: www.icj-cij.org/en/how-the-court-works

International Court of Justice. "Maritime delimitations in the Indian Ocean (Somalia v. Kenya)," 2021. Available at: www.icj-cij.org/public/files/case-related/161/161-20211012-JUD-01-00-EN.pdf

International Court of Justice. "Nicaragua v. United States of America: Merits," 1986. Available at: www.icj-cij.org/public/files/case-related/70/070-19860627-JUD-01-00-EN.pdf

International Court of Justice. "Summary of the Advisory Opinion," 2004. Available at: www.icj-cij.org/public/files/case-related/131/1677.pdf

International Court of Justice. "Ukraine v. Russian Federation," 2022b. Available at: www.icj-cij.org/public/files/case-related/182/182-20220316-ORD-01-00-EN.pdf

International Criminal Court. "Decision on the 'Prosecution request pursuant to article 19(3) for a ruling on the Court's territorial jurisdiction in Palestine'," 2021. Available at: www.icc-cpi.int/Pages/record.aspx?docNo=ICC-01/18-143

International Criminal Court. "How the court works," 2022. Available at: www. icc-cpi.int/about/how-the-court-works

International Criminal Court. "Situation in Palestine | summary of preliminary examination findings," 2020. Available at: www.icc-cpi.int/itemsDocuments/ 210303-office-of-the-prosecutor-palestine-summary-findings-eng.pdf

Jenkins, Loren. "World court says U.S. violates international law by aiding contras." *Washington Post*, 1986. Available at: https://www.washingtonpost.com/ archive/politics/1986/06/28/world-court-says-us-violates-international-law-by-aiding-contras/8aedb6b7-4461-4686-b5e5-af9870028751/

Johnson, Hayley. "#NoDAPL: Social media, empowerment, and civic participation at standing rock." *Library Trends* 66, no. 2 (2017): 155–175.

Joseph, Sarah. "Protracted lawfare: The tale of Chevron Texaco in the Amazon." *Journal of Human Rights and the Environment* 3, no. 1 (2012): 70–91.

Justice, Jeff. "Of guns and ballots: Attitudes towards unconventional and destructive political participation among Sinn Féin and Herri Batasuna supporters." *Nationalism and Ethnic Politics* 11, no. 3 (2005): 295–320.

Kant, Immanuel. *Perpetual Peace: A Philosophical Sketch*. The Macmillan Company, 1795/1917. Available at: http://files.libertyfund.org/files/357/0075_Bk.pdf

Karagiannis, Emmanuel. "The Russian interventions in South Ossetia and Crimea compared: Military performance, legitimacy and goals." *Contemporary Security Policy* 35, no. 3 (2014): 400–420.

Kelemen, Daniel and Mitchell Orenstein. "Europe's autocracy problem. Polish democracy's final days?" *Foreign Affairs*, 2016. Available at: www.foreignaffairs. com/articles/poland/2016-01-07/europes-autocracy-problem

Kelsen, Hans. *Peace Through Law*. The Lawbook Exchange, 1944/2000.

Kelsen, Hans. *Pure Theory of Law*. University of California Press, 1967.

Kennedy, David. "Lawfare and warfare." In *The Cambridge Companion to International Law*, edited by James Crawford and Martti Koskenniemi, 158–184. Cambridge University Press, 2012.

Kennedy, David. *Of War and Law*. Princeton University Press, 2006.

Keohane, Robert O., Andrew Moravcsik and Anne-Marie Slaughter. "Legalized dispute resolution: Interstate and transnational." *International Organization* 54, no. 3 (2000): 457–488.

Kiely, Ray. "From authoritarian liberalism to economic technocracy: Neoliberalism, politics and 'de-democratization'." *Critical Sociology* 43, nos. 4–5 (2017): 725–745.

Kirchheimer, Otto. *Political Justice: The Use of Legal Procedure for Political Ends*. Princeton University Press, 2015.

Kissinger, Henry. "The pitfalls of universal jurisdiction." *Foreign Affairs* 80 (2001): 86–96.

Kittrie, Orde F. *Lawfare: Law as a Weapon of War*. Oxford University Press, 2016.

Konkes, Claire. "Green lawfare: Environmental public interest litigation and mediatized environmental conflict." *Environmental Communication* 12, no. 2 (2018): 191–203.

Kramarz, T., Cosolo, D. and Rossi, A. "Judicialization of environmental policy and the crisis of democratic accountability." *Review of Policy Research* 34, no. 1 (2017): 31–49.

Kremlin. "Address by president of the Russian Federation," 2014. Available at: http://en.kremlin.ru/events/president/news/20603

Kremlin. "National security strategy of the Russian Federation," 2021. Available at: www.kremlin.ru/acts/bank/47046

Ku, Julian G. "Kiobel and the surprising death of universal jurisdiction under the Alien Tort Statute." *American Journal of International Law* 107, no. 4 (2013): 835–841.

Kuperman, Alan J. "Obama's Libya debacle: How a well-meaning intervention ended in failure." *Foreign Affairs* 94, no. 2 (2015): 66–77.

Landau, David. "Abusive constitutionalism." *U.C. Davis Law Review* 47, no. 1 (2013): 189–260.

League of Nations. "The Covenant of the League of Nations," 1919. Available at: https://avalon.law.yale.edu/20th_century/leagcov.asp#art16

Lee, Sangkuk. "China's 'three warfares': Origins, applications, and organizations." *Journal of Strategic Studies* 37, no. 2 (2014): 198–221.

Lehoucq, Emilio, and Whitney K. Taylor. "Conceptualizing legal mobilization: How should we understand the deployment of legal strategies?" *Law & Social Inquiry* 45, no. 1 (2020): 166–193.

Lin, Jolene. "Climate change and the courts." *Legal Studies* 32, no. 1 (2012): 35–57.

Lorde, Audre. *The Master's Tools Will Never Dismantle the Master's House*. Penguin, 2018.

Lowry, David. "Internment in Northern Ireland." *University of Toledo Law Review* 8, no. 1 (1976): 169–208.

Mackinnon, Amy. "Russia's Wagner Group doesn't actually exist." *Foreign Policy*, 2021. Available at: https://foreignpolicy.com/2021/07/06/what-is-wagner-group-russia-mercenaries-military-contractor/

Marten, Kimberly. "Russia's use of semi-state security forces: The case of the Wagner Group." *Post-Soviet Affairs* 35, no. 3 (2019): 181–204.

Marx, Karl, and Friedrich Engels. *The Communist Manifesto*. Appleton Century Crofts, 1955.

McGarry, John. "Explaining ethnonationalism: The flaws in western thinking." *Nationalism and Ethnic Politics* 1, no. 4 (1995): 121–142.

McGinn, Colin. *Philosophical Provocations: 55 Short Essays*. MIT Press, 2017.

Mearsheimer, John J. "The inevitable rivalry: America, China, and the tragedy of great-power politics." *Foreign Affairs* 100 (2021): 48–59.

Mezey, Naomi. "It's not just Catalan separatists. Democracy is also on trial in Spain." *The Washington Post*, 2019. Available at: www.washingtonpost.com/

opinions/2019/02/12/its-not-just-catalan-separatists-democracy-is-also-trial-spain/

Michel, Jean-Baptiste, Yuan Kui Shen, Aviva Presser Aiden, Adrian Veres, Matthew K. Gray, Google Books Team, Joseph P. Pickett, et al. "Quantitative analysis of culture using millions of digitized books." *Science* 331, no. 6014 (2011): 176–182.

Moore, John. "Jus ad bellum before the International Court of Justice." *Virginia Journal of International Law* 52, no. 4 (2012): 903–962.

Morgenthau, Hans J. "An intellectual autobiography." *Society* 15, no. 2 (1978): 63–68.

Morgenthau, Hans J. *In Defense of the National interest: A Critical Examination of American Foreign Policy.* Alfred Knopf, 1951.

Morgenthau, Hans J. *Politics among Nations.* McGraw-Hill Education, 1948/2005.

Moroska-Bonkiewicz, Aleksandra and Angela Bourne. "The impact of the past on contemporary responses to political extremism: The cases of Poland and Spain." *Journal of Contemporary European Studies* 28, no. 4 (2020): 464–476.

Morrissey, John. "Liberal lawfare and biopolitics: US juridical warfare in the war on terror." *Geopolitics* 16, no. 2 (2011): 280–305.

MOSOP. "Ogoni Bill of Rights," 2015. Available at: www.mosop.org/2015/10/10/ogoni-bill-of-rights/

Mouawad, Jad. "Shell to pay $15.5 million to settle Nigerian case." *New York Times*, 2009. Available at: www.nytimes.com/2009/06/09/business/global/09shell.html

Moustafa, Tamir and Tom Ginsburg. "Introduction: The Functions of Courts in Authoritarian Politics." In *Rule by Law: The Politics of Courts in Authoritarian Regimes*, edited by Tom Ginsburg and Tamir Moustafa, 1–22. Cambridge University Press, 2008.

Munoz Mosquera, Andres and Sascha Dov Bachmann. "Lawfare in hybrid wars: The 21st century warfare." *Journal of International Humanitarian Legal Studies* 7, no. 1 (2016): 63–87.

Munoz Mosquera, Andres, Sascha Dov Bachmann and J. Abraham Munoz Bravo. "Hybrid warfare and the legal domain." *Terrorism and Political Violence* 31, no. 1 (2019): 98–104.

Murua, Imanol. "No more bullets for ETA: The loss of internal support as a key factor in the end of the Basque group's campaign." *Critical Studies on Terrorism* 10, no. 1 (2017): 93–114.

Nephew, Richard. *The Art of Sanctions.* Columbia University Press, 2017.

Newton, Michael A. "Illustrating illegitimate lawfare." *Case Western Reserve Journal of International Law* 43 (2010): 255–279.

Northern Ireland Office. "The Belfast agreement," 1998. Available at: www.gov.uk/government/publications/the-belfast-agreement

Nye, Joseph S. "Soft power." *Foreign Policy* 80 (1990): 153–171.

Nye, Joseph S. "Soft power: The origins and political progress of a concept." *The Journal of International Communication* (2021): 1–7.

Obi, Cyril I. "Globalisation and local resistance: The case of the Ogoni versus Shell." *New Political Economy* 2, no. 1 (1997): 137–148.

O'Boyle, Michael. "Torture and emergency powers under the European Convention on human rights: Ireland v. the United Kingdom." *American Journal of International Law* 71, no. 4 (1977): 674–706.

O'Dochartaigh, Niall. *From Civil Rights to Armalites: Derry and the Birth of the Irish Troubles*. Palgrave, 2005.

O'Doherty, Malachi. *The Trouble with Guns: Republican Strategy and the Provisional IRA*. Blackstaff Press, 1997.

Odom, Jonathan G. "A China in the bull shop? Comparing the rhetoric of a rising China with the reality of the international law of the sea." *Ocean & Coastal Law Journal* 17, no. 2 (2011): 201–252.

O'Donnell, Guillermo. "The quality of democracy: Why the rule of law matters." *Journal of Democracy* 15, no. 4 (2004): 32–46.

Official Journal of the European Union. "Council common position 2009/468/ CFSP," 2009. Available at: https://eur-lex.europa.eu/legal-content/EN/TXT/ PDF/?uri=CELEX:32009E0468&qid=1412596355797&from=EN

Østensen, Åse Gilje and Tor Bukkvoll. "Private military companies – Russian great power politics on the cheap?" *Small Wars & Insurgencies* 33, no. 1–2 (2022): 130–151.

PACE. "The definition of political prisoner," 2012. Available at: https://assembly. coe.int/nw/xml/XRef/Xref-XML2HTML-en.asp?fileid=19150&lang=en

Pappas, George D. *The Literary and Legal Genealogy of Native American Dispossession: The Marshall Trilogy Cases*. Routledge, 2017.

Pattison, James. *The Alternatives to War: From Sanctions to Nonviolence*. Oxford University Press, 2018.

Pattison, James. *The Morality of Private War: The Challenge of Private Military and Security Companies*. Oxford University Press, 2014.

Peel, Jacqueline and Jolene Lin. "Transnational climate litigation: The contribution of the global south." *American Journal of International Law* 113, no. 4 (2019): 679–726.

Pegg, Scott. "Feature review Ken Saro-Wiwa: Assessing the multiple legacies of a literary interventionist." *Third World Quarterly* 21, no. 4 (2000): 701–708.

Permanent Court of Arbitration. "The South China Sea Arbitration (The Republic of Philippines v. The People's Republic of China)," 2016. Available at: https:// pcacases.com/web/sendAttach/1801

Philippine's Foreign Ministry. "Notification and statement of claim," 2013. Available at: https://dfa.gov.ph/images/UNCLOS/Notification%20and% 20Statement%20of%20Claim%20on%20West%20Philippine%20Sea.pdf

Phillips, Tom. "Bolsonaro appoints judge who helped jail Lula to lead justice ministry." *The Guardian*, 2018. Available at: www.theguardian.com/world/2018/ nov/01/bolsonaro-sergio-moro-brazil-justice-ministry-anti-corruption

Pogies, Christian. "Oceans of cynicism? Norm-genesis, lawfare and the South China Sea arbitration case." In *Cynical International Law?*, edited by Björnstjern Baade, Dana Burchardt, Prisca Feihle, Alicia Köppen, Linus Mührel, Lena Riemer and Raphael Schäfer, 143–162. Springer, 2021.

Portela, Clara. "Countering the extraterritorial effects of US sanctions." *European Union Institute for Security Studies* 22 (2021): 1–8.

Potter, Ben. "Brandis crackdown on green activist lawsuits could aid Shenhua mine." *Australian Financial Review*, 2015. Available at: www.afr.com/companies/ mining/brandis-crackdown-on-green-activist-lawsuits-could-aid-shenhua-mine-20150816-gj013c

Przybylski, Wojciech. "Explaining Eastern Europe: Can Poland's backsliding be stopped?" *Journal of Democracy* 29, no. 3 (2018): 52–64.

Przybylski, Wojciech. "The end of the Budapest–Warsaw axis." *Politico*, 2022. Available at: www.politico.eu/article/hungary-poland-axis-diplomacy-ukraine-russia-war-vikto0r-orban-fidesz-pis-visegrad-group/

Qiao, Liang, and Xiangsui Wang. *Unrestricted Warfare*. PLA Literature and Arts Publishing House, 1999.

Qureshi, Wassem. "Lawfare: The weaponization of international law." *Houston Journal of International Law* 42, no. 1 (2019): 39–85.

Radan, Peter. "Secessionist referenda in international and domestic law." *Nationalism and Ethnic Politics* 18, no. 1 (2012): 8–21.

Radil, Steven M. "South China Sea Map," 2022.

Randeria, Shalini. "De-politicization of democracy and judicialization of politics." *Theory, Culture & Society* 24, no. 4 (2007): 38–44.

Reuters. "Philippines says won't protest China actions in Spratly Islands," 2016. Available at: www.reuters.com/article/southchinasea-philippines-china-idINKBN1450WL

Ribeiro, Ricardo Lodi. "Lula's conviction: Brazil's most striking case of lawfare." In *Comments on a Notorious Verdict: The Trial of Lula*, edited by Carol Proner, Gisele Cittadino, Gisele Ricobom and João Ricardo Dornelles, 182–185. Consejo Latinoamericano de Ciencias Sociales, 2018.

Rishikof, Harvey. "Juridical warfare: The neglected legal instrument." *Joint Force Quarterly* 48, no. 1 (2008): 11–13.

Robinson, Kali. "Yemen's tragedy: War, stalemate, and suffering." *Council on Foreign Relations*, 2022. Available at: www.cfr.org/backgrounder/yemen-crisis

Romano, Silvina. "Lawfare y neoliberalismo en América Latina: una aproximación." *Sudamérica: Revista de Ciencias Sociales* 13 (2020): 14–40.

Rosland, Sissel. "Victimhood, identity, and agency in the early phase of the troubles in Northern Ireland." *Identities* 16, no. 3 (2009): 294–320.

Roth, Kenneth. "The case for universal jurisdiction." *Foreign Affairs* (2001): 150–154.

Rousseau, Kevin. "International law and military strategy: Changes in the strategic operating environment." *Journal of National Security Law and Policy* 9 (2017): 1–17.

Rousseff, Dilma. "Lawfare contra Lula." *Twitter*, 2020. Available at: https://twitter.com/dilmabr/status/1299428899680653314

Ruggie, John Gerard. "Multinationals as global institution: Power, authority and relative autonomy." *Regulation & Governance* 12, no. 3 (2018): 317–333.

Ruggie, John Gerard. "Reconstituting the global public domain – issues, actors, and practices." *European Journal of International Relations* 10, no. 4 (2004): 499–531.

Russian Ministry of Foreign Affairs. "Foreign ministry statement," 2018. Available at: https://archive.mid.ru/en/web/guest/maps/ua/-asset_publisher/ktn0ZLTvbbS3/content/id/3414549

Russian Ministry of Foreign Affairs. "The foreign policy concept of the Russian Federation," 2016. Available at: www.rusemb.org.uk/rp_insight/

Sadurski, Wojciech. "How democracy dies (in Poland): A case study of anti-constitutional populist backsliding." *Sydney Law School, Legal Studies Research Paper* 18, no. 1 (2018): 1–71.

Said, Edward. "The treason of the Intellectuals." In *Masters of the Universe?: NATO's Balkan Crusade*, edited by Tariq Ali, et al., 341–344. Verso, 2000.

Sallon, Hélène. "The judicialization of politics in Israel. Promoting Arab collective claims in the judicial arena." *Bulletin Du Centre de Recherche Français à Jérusalem*, no. 16 (2005): 287–300.

Sánchez-Cuenca, Ignacio. "Power, rules, and compliance." In *Democracy and the Rule of Law*, edited by Adam Przeworski and José María Maravall, 62–93. Cambridge University Press, 2003.

Santora, Marc. "Poland purges Supreme Court, and protesters take to streets." *New York Times*, 2018. Available at: www.nytimes.com/2018/07/03/world/europe/poland-supreme-court-protest.html

Sare'e, Yahya. "Yemeni armed forces communiqué." *Twitter*, 2022. Available at: https://twitter.com/Yahya_Saree/status/1477941881413767170

Sari, Aurel. "Legal resilience in an era of grey zone conflicts and hybrid threats." *Cambridge Review of International Affairs* 33, no. 6 (2020): 846–867.

Saro-Wiwa, Ken. *A Month and a Day – A Detention Diary*. Penguin, 1995.

Saunt, Claudio. *Unworthy Republic: The Dispossession of Native Americans and the Road to Indian Territory*. W.W. Norton & Company, 2020.

Savaresi, Annalisa, and Juan Auz. "Climate change litigation and human rights: Pushing the boundaries." *Climate Law* 9, no. 3 (2019): 244–262.

Schaeffer, Robert K. *Severed States: Dilemmas of Democracy in a Divided World*. Rowman & Littlefield, 1999.

Schmitt, Carl. *Legality and Legitimacy*. Duke University Press, 1932/2004.

Schmitt, Michael N. "Wings over Libya: The no-fly zone in legal perspective." *Yale Journal of International Law Online* 36 (2011): 45–58.

Schrempf-Stirling, Judith, and Florian Wettstein. "Beyond guilty verdicts: Human rights litigation and its impact on corporations' human rights policies." *Journal of Business Ethics* 145, no. 3 (2017): 545–562.

Scott, James C. *Weapons of the Weak: Everyday Forms of Peasant Resistance*. Yale University Press, 1985. Available at: http://archive.org/details/weaponsofweakeve0000scot

Searle, John R. "Constitutive rules." *Argumenta* 4, no. 1 (2018): 51–54.

Setzer, Joana and Catherine Higham. "Global trends in climate change litigation: 2021 snapshot." *London School of Economics and Political Science* (2021): 1–45. Available at: https://www.lse.ac.uk/granthaminstitute/wp-content/uploads/2021/07/Global-trends-in-climate-change-litigation_2021-snapshot.pdf

Setzer, Joana and Lisa C. Vanhala. "Climate change litigation: A review of research on courts and litigants in climate governance." *Wiley Interdisciplinary Reviews: Climate Change* 10, no. 3 (2019): 1–19.

Shamir, Ronen. "The de-radicalization of corporate social responsibility." *Critical Sociology* 30, no. 3 (2004): 669–689.

Slaughter, Anne-Marie. "Judicial globalization." *Virginia Journal of International Law* 40 (1999): 1103.

Smith, M. L. R. *Fighting for Ireland?: The Military Strategy of the Irish Republican Movement*. Routledge, 1997.

Smith, William. *The British State and the Northern Ireland Crisis, 1969–73: From Violence to Power Sharing.* US Institute of Peace Press, 2011.

Sólyom, László. "The rise and decline of constitutional culture in Hungary." In *Constitutional Crisis in the European Constitutional Area. Theory, Law and Politics in Hungary and Romania,* edited by Armin von Bogdandy and Pál Sonnevend, 14–45. CH Beck – Hart – Nomos, 2015.

Southern District Court NY. "Wiwa vs. Royal Dutch Petroleum Company," 1996. Available at: https://ccrjustice.org/sites/default/files/assets/11.8.96%20%20Wiwa%20Complaint.pdf

Spanish Constitutional Court. "Sentencia 114/2017", 2017. Available at: https://www.boe.es/boe/dias/2017/10/24/pdfs/BOE-A-2017-12206.pdf

Spanish Ministry of Interior. "La Policía descabeza de nuevo a Askatasuna, parte esencial del entramado de ETA," 2003. Available at: https://www.interior.gob.es/opencms/es/detalle/articulo/La-Policia-descabeza-de-nuevo-a-Askatasuna-parte-esencial-del-entramado-de-ETA/

Spector, Regine. "Property, lawfare, and the politics of hope in weak states." *Polity* 51, no. 1 (2019): 3–34.

Steinman, Erich. "Why was Standing Rock and the #NoDAPL campaign so historic? Factors affecting American Indian participation in social movement collaborations and coalitions." *Ethnic and Racial Studies* 42, no. 7 (2019): 1070–1090.

Striffler, Steve. "Correa's trial is an attack on Ecuador's democracy", *Al Jazeera,* 2020. Available at: https://www.aljazeera.com/opinions/2020/6/2/correas-trial-is-an-attack-on-ecuadors-democracy

Suchman, Mark C. "Managing legitimacy: Strategic and institutional approaches." *Academy of Management Review* 20, no. 3 (1995): 571–610.

Sunkin, Maurice. "Judicialization of Politics in the United Kingdom." *International Political Science Review* 15, no. 2 (1994): 125–133.

Terry, Patrick CR. "Letter to the journal unilateral economic sanctions and their extraterritorial impact: One foreign policy for all?," *Chinese Journal of International Law* 18, no. 2 (2019): 425–435.

The Economist. "Viktor Orban's visit to Warsaw showcased an illiberal alliance," 2018. Available at: www.economist.com/europe/2018/05/17/viktor-orbans-visit-to-warsaw-showcased-an-illiberal-alliance

Thirlway, Hugh. "Territorial disputes and their resolution in the recent jurisprudence of the International Court of Justice." *Leiden Journal of International Law* 31, no. 1 (2018): 117–146.

Tiemessen, Alana. "The International Criminal Court and the lawfare of judicial intervention." *International Relations* 30, no. 4 (2016): 409–431.

Tirado, Arantxa. *El lawfare: Golpes de Estado en nombre de la ley.* Ediciones Akal, 2021.

Tóka, Gábor. "Constitutional principles and electoral democracy in Hungary." In *Verfassunggebung in Konsolidierten Demokratien,* edited by Ellen Bos and Kálmán Pòcza, 309–329. Nomos Verlagsgesellschaft, 2014.

Trachtman, Joel. "Integrating lawfare and warfare." *Boston College International & Comparative Law Review* 39, no. 2 (2016): 267–282.

Triffler, Steve. "Correa's trial is an attack on Ecuador's democracy." *Al Jazeera*, 2020. Available at: www.aljazeera.com/opinions/2020/6/2/correas-trial-is-an-attack-on-ecuadors-democracy

Tropin, Zakhar. "Lawfare as part of hybrid wars: The experience of Ukraine in conflict with the Russian Federation." *Security and Defence Quarterly* 33, no. 1 (2021): 15–29.

Tsebelis, George. "Decision making in political systems: Veto players in presidentialism, parlamentarism, multicameralism and multipartism." *British Journal of Political Science* 25 (1995): 289–325.

Tysiachniouk, Maria S., Leah S. Horowitz, Varvara V. Korkina and Andrey N. Petrov. "Indigenous-led grassroots engagements with oil pipelines in the U.S. and Russia: The NoDAPL and komi movements." *Environmental Politics* 30, no. 6 (2021): 895–917.

Ukrainian Ministry of Foreign Affairs. "Russia opens the third front of aggression," 2018. Available at: https://iraq.mfa.gov.ua/en/news/69207-russia-opens-the-third-front-of-aggression-against-ukraine-in-the-azovblack-sea-region

United Nations. "A/RES/63/3," 2008. Available at: https://digitallibrary.un.org/record/637746?ln=en

United Nations. "Map no. 3773 Rev. 6," 2014. Available at: https://www.un.org/geospatial/sites/www.un.org.geospatial/files/files/documents/2020/Apr/ukraine_3773_r6_mar14_120.pdf

United Nations. "Note Verbale from the Permanent Mission of the PRC to the UN CML/42/2020," 2020a. Available at: www.un.org/Depts/los/clcs_new/submissions_files/mys_12_12_2019/2020_04_17_CHN_NV_UN_003_EN.pdf

United Nations. "Paris Agreement," 2015. Available at: https://unfccc.int/sites/default/files/english_paris_agreement.pdf

United Nations. "Permanent mission of the Commonwealth of Australia to the United Nations N° 20/026," 2020b. Available at: www.un.org/depts/los/clcs_new/submissions_files/mys_12_12_2019/2020_07_23_AUS_NV_UN_001_OLA-2020-00373.pdf

United Nations. "The United Nations Convention on the Law of the Sea," 1982. Available at: www.un.org/depts/los/convention_agreements/texts/unclos/unclos_e.pdf

United Nations. "UN Charter," 1945. Available at: www.un.org/en/about-us/un-charter

United Nations. "United Nations Security Council S/RES/1973," 2011. Available at: www.un.org/securitycouncil/s/res/1973-%282011%29

United Nations. "United Nations Security Council S/RES/661," 1990. Available at: http://unscr.com/en/resolutions/doc/661

United Nations. "United Nations Security Council S/RES/661," 2002. Available at: www.un.org/Depts/unmovic/documents/1441.pdf

University of Minnesota. "Princeton principles on universal jurisdiction," 2001. Available at: http://hrlibrary.umn.edu/instree/princeton.html

Urías Martínez, Joaquín Pablo. "El artículo 155 CE: alcance y límites de una excepción constitucional." *Revista Catalana de Dret Públic* special issue, (2019): 101–114.

Urías Martínez, Joaquín Pablo. "Spain has a problem with its judiciary." *Verfassungsblog*, 2020. Available at: https://verfassungsblog.de/spain-has-a-problem-with-its-judiciary/

US Congress. "H.R.5237 - Native American Graves Protection and Repatriation Act", 1990. Available at: https://www.congress.gov/bill/101st-congress/house-bill/5237#:~:text=Passed%20Senate%20amended%20(10%2F26,on%20Federal%20or%20tribal%20lands

US Constitution. "Article IV § 3", 1787. Available at: www.archives.gov/founding-docs/constitution-transcript

US Department of Defense. "Military and security developments involving the PRC," 2021. Available at: https://media.defense.gov/2021/Nov/03/2002885874/-1/-1/0/2021-CMPR-FINAL.PDF

US Department of Defense. "National defense strategy," 2005. Available at: https://history.defense.gov/Portals/70/Documents/nds/2005_NDS.pdf?ver=tFA4Qqo94ZB0x_S6uL0QEg%3d%3d

US Department of Justice. "United States of America vs. Huawei Technologies," 2019 Available at: www.justice.gov/usao-edny/press-release/file/1125036/download

US Department of State. "Limits in the seas: People's Republic of China: Maritime claims in the South China Sea," 2022. Available at: www.state.gov/wp-content/uploads/2022/01/LIS150-SCS.pdf

US Department of State. "U.S. Withdrawal from the proceedings initiated by Nicaragua in the ICJ," 1985. Available at: www.jstor.org/stable/pdf/20692794.pdf

US Department of Treasury. "Sanction programs and country information," 2022b. Available at: https://home.treasury.gov/policy-issues/financial-sanctions/sanctions-programs-and-country-information

US Department of Treasury. "Sanctions list search," 2022a. Available at: https://sanctionssearch.ofac.treas.gov/

US Department of Treasury. "U.S. Treasury announces unprecedented & expansive sanctions against Russia, imposing swift and severe economic costs," 2022c. Available at: https://home.treasury.gov/news/press-releases/jy0608

US Navy. "7th Fleet conducts freedom of navigation operation," 2021. Available at: www.navy.mil/Press-Office/News-Stories/Article/2766828/7th-fleet-conducts-freedom-of-navigation-operation/

US Supreme Court. "*Cherokee Nation v. Georgia*," 1831. Available at: https://supreme.justia.com/cases/federal/us/30/1/

US Supreme Court. "*Johnson v. McIntosh*," 1823. Available at: https://supreme.justia.com/cases/federal/us/21/543/

US Supreme Court. "*Kiobel v. Royal Dutch Petroleum*," 2013. Available at: www.supremecourt.gov/opinions/12pdf/10-1491_l6gn.pdf

US Supreme Court. "*United States v. Kagama*," 1886. Available at: https://supreme.justia.com/cases/federal/us/118/375/

US Supreme Court. "*Worcester v. Georgia*," 1832. Available at: https://supreme. justia.com/cases/federal/us/31/515/

Vallejo, Catalina and Siri Gloppen. "Red-green lawfare? Climate change narratives in courtrooms." In *Climate Talk: Right, Poverty and Justice*, edited by Jackie Dugard, Asuncion Lera St. Clair and Siri Gloppen, 208–235. Juta, 2013.

Vanhala, Lisa. "Legal opportunity structures and the paradox of legal mobilization by the environmental movement in the UK." *Journal Law and Society* 46, no. 3 (2012): 523–556.

Vollenweider, Camila and Silvina Romano. "Lawfare. La Judicialización de La Política En América Latina." *Centro Estratégico Latinoamericano de Geopolítica (CELAG)*, 2017. Available at: www.celag.org/wp-content/uploads/2017/03/LawfareT.pdf

Von Staden, Andreas. *Strategies of Compliance with the European Court of Human Rights*. University of Pennsylvania Press, 2018.

Wæver, Ole. "Securitization and desecuritization." *Centre for Peace and Conflict Research* 5, (1993): 1–31.

Wagner Group. "About us," 2022. Available at: https://wagnera.ru/

Walsh, Dermot PJ. *Bloody Sunday and the Rule of Law in Northern Ireland*. Palgrave Macmillan, 2000.

Wang, Dong. *China's Unequal Treaties: Narrating National History*. Lexington Books, 2005.

Warnes, R. and G. Hannah. "Meeting the challenge of extremist and radicalized prisoners: The experiences of the United Kingdom and Spain." *Policing* 2, no. 4 (2008): 402–411.

Weber, Max. *Economy and Society: An Outline of Interpretive Sociology*. University of California Press, 1922/1978.

Wedgwood, Ruth. "International criminal law and Augusto Pinochet." *Vancouver Journal of International Law* 40 (1999): 829–848.

Weiss, Thomas G. "Sanctions as a foreign policy tool: Weighing humanitarian impulses." *Journal of Peace Research* 36, no. 5 (1999): 499–509.

Weizman, Eyal. "Legislative attack." *Theory, Culture & Society* 27, no. 6 (2010): 11–32.

Werner, Wouter. "The curious career of lawfare." *Case Western Reserve Journal of International Law* 43, no. 1 (2010): 61–72.

Wheeler, Nicholas J. "Reflections on the legality and legitimacy of NATO's intervention in Kosovo." *The International Journal of Human Rights* 4, no. 3–4 (2000): 144–163.

Whitfield, Teresa. *Endgame for ETA: Elusive peace in the Basque Country*. Oxford University Press, 2014.

White House. "Imposing sanctions with respect to Iran," 2019. Available at: www.govinfo.gov/content/pkg/FR-2019-06-26/pdf/2019-13793.pdf

White House. "Interim National Security Strategic Guidance," 2021. Available at: www.whitehouse.gov/wp-content/uploads/2021/03/NSC-1v2.pdf

White House. "National security strategy of the United States of America," 2017. Available at: https://history.defense.gov/Portals/70/Documents/nss/NSS2017. pdf?ver=CnFwURrw09pJ0q5EogFpwg%3d%3d

White, Robert W. and Terry Falkenberg White. "Repression and the liberal state: The case of Northern Ireland, 1969–1972." *Journal of Conflict Resolution* 39, no. 2 (1995): 330–352.

Wildhaber, Luzius. "The European Court of Human Rights in action." *Ritsumeikan Law Review* 21 (2004): 83–92.

Wilson, Woodrow. *Addresses of President Wilson*. US Government Printing Office, 1919.

Winkler, Adam. *We the Corporations: How American Businesses Won Their Civil Rights*. Liveright Publishing, 2018.

Woodworth, Paddy. "The Spanish-Basque peace process: How to get things wrong." *World Policy Journal* 24, no. 1 (2007): 65–73.

Zakaria, Fareed. *The Future of Freedom: Illiberal Democracy at Home and Abroad*. WW Norton & Company, 2003.

Zanin, Cristiano, Valeska Martins and Rafael Valim. *Lawfare: Waging War through Law*. Routledge, 2021.

Zárate, Juan. *Treasury's War: The Unleashing of a New Era of Financial Warfare*. Hachette, 2013.

Zhao, Suisheng. "The US–China rivalry in the emerging bipolar world: Hostility, alignment, and power balance." *Journal of Contemporary China* 31, no. 134 (2022): 169–185.

Zhihao, Zhang. "PLA issues warning after US warship enters territorial waters." *China Daily*, 2021. Available at: www.chinadaily.com.cn/a/202105/20/WS60a5f743a31024ad0bac04cd.html

Zieliński, Tadeusz. "On theory and practice of no-fly zones in humanitarian intervention." *Studies in Conflict & Terrorism* (2021): 1–18.

Index

Note: Figures are denoted with italicised page numbers. End note information is denoted by n and note number following the page number.

For Product Safety Concerns and Information please contact our EU
representative GPSR@taylorandfrancis.com Taylor & Francis Verlag GmbH,
Kaufingerstraße 24, 80331 München, Germany

Printed and bound by CPI Group (UK) Ltd, Croydon, CR0 4YY
11/04/2025
01844010-0011